IKIGAI

WHAT MAKES LIFE WORTH LIVING. FIND YOUR PURPOSE IN LIFE THANKS TO THE ESSENTIAL JAPANESE WAY

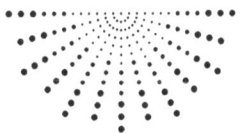

ISABELLA MALES

CONTENTS

INTRODUCTION	1
1. WHY CHANGE YOUR LIFE PERSPECTIVE?	9
Beginnings Of Negative Reasoning	10
2. SIMPLIFY	14
Focus on what makes the biggest difference to you	15
Can we say that you are trapped in an economic cycle?	16
Improve on your life	17
Work on your life, time, and schedules	18
Begin by recognizing the areas of stress	18
3. THE BENEFITS OF MEDITATION	21
4. ZEN MEDITATION	26
Contemplation procedures	29
5. WHAT IS IKIGAI	31
Could you understand Ikigai?	31
6. THE FIVE PILLARS OF IKIGAI TO RECONNECT WITH YOURSELF	34
Activity	36
7. FLOW	37
Be where you are and live in that time	38
8. COVERING YOUR REASON FOR BEING	43
9. ACHIEVING IKIGAI	45
7 is the enchanted number	46
Did I say seven is wizardry?	47
10. HOW TO FIND MOTIVATION	50
Track down your call	52
Save the world	52
Look forward	54

11.	ENJOYING EVERY DAY FOLLOWING THE 5 PILLARS	55
12.	THE CONCEPT OF WABI SABI	57
13.	MANDALAS	60
	Mandala imagery	61
	The holy significance of the Mandala	62
	Development of the priests Mandala	62
	How to draw your Mandala?	64
	Draw Mandalas without any problem	66
	The five Buddha families and their tones	68
	What are the purposes of a Mandala?	69
	Tips for a mandala for treatment	70
	Realities about the Mandala	71
14.	A ONE MINUTE MEDITATION YOU CAN DO ANYWHERE	94
	The most effective way to do a brief reflection	94
15.	THE LONG ROAD OF IKIGAI	96
	How might IKIGAI help us?	97
	Estimating the IKIGAI survey	98
	So how could it be estimated?	98
	IKIGAI-9 poll	98
	By what other means could we quantify the IKIGAI	99
	Fulfillment with the stepping stool of life	100
	Individuals who are very disappointed with their life	101
	4 tests you can utilize	101
	Track down your motivation	103
16.	TIPS FOR ACHIEVING IKIGAI	106
17.	HOW TO FIND YOUR IDEAL JOB WITH THE IKIGAI METHOD	109
	A little foundation data	109
	Applying it to the expert region	110
18.	REDISCOVERING THE PASSION FOR WORK	113
	For what reason does IKIGAI resound with so many?	114
	Apply IKIGAI to your profession	115

19. EXERCISES	116
What were your beloved activities as a teen?	117
Rundown of subjects	119
20. THE IKIGAI DIET	121
Japanese superfoods	122
Wayasahii Wizard: My grandchildren are caring	123
It's not just about food	125
21. THE SECRETS OF THE OKINAWANS	126
So what's their mystery?	127
What is Moai?	127
What is HaraHachiBu?	128
22. EXERCISES TO IMPROVE YOUR IMMUNE SYSTEM	130
Japanese IKIGAI works out	132
Activities of Radio Taiso	133
Radio Taiso	134
Stretch and develop	134
Stretch 'n' Grow Radio Taiso	134
23. PRACTICE TAI CHI QUAN TO INCREASE LONGEVITY	137
CONCLUSIONS	142
The longest-lived individuals	144
Did you track down your IKIGAI?	145

Copyright © 2022 Isabella Males

All rights reserved. No part of this publication may be reproduced, distributed, or transmitted in any form or by any means, including photocopying, recording, or other electronic or mechanical methods, without the prior written permission of the publisher, except in the case of brief quotations embodied in critical reviews and certain other non-commercial uses permitted by copyright law.

INTRODUCTION

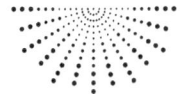

The Japanese have a unique word for the sensation of reviewing life as having a purpose. This term does not exist in the West. If the individual doesn't see this importance in their reality, they don't have the foggiest idea of what they are living for, because they have an unfilled existence consistently once more, intelligently they have less energy and joy than individuals who have perceived their motivation in the daily routine and who structure their daily experiences to do satisfying things that bring them joy and fulfillment.

Every individual feels somewhere deep in their heart the desire for a meaningful life. Sooner or later in our life, each of us is confronted with the subject of the importance of life. We may not pose the inquiry rationally. All things being equal, we could ask ourselves: what am I doing here on the planet? Why am I here? A considerable lot of us don't track down the responses, or simply think that they are insufficient. Let's face it: What answers do we get when we ask our companions for what valid reason they get up toward the beginning of the day? Also, who can see us more or less what their motivation in life comprises of? Frequently, we feel vulnerable notwithstanding questions like these on the grounds that we surely need to know the responses, however, we can't. Additionally, some people might respond with dismay because the survey hints at their agonizing lack of motivation and life seeming senseless or intentional.

The Japanese standard of IKIGAI can shockingly help us determine the importance of our routine, in light of the fact that each of us has IKIGAI. It is therefore certainly worth engaging in a specific quest for meaning. I wish you many enlightening accomplishments and much happiness along the way. Also, I generally wish you a lot of IKIGAI.

Imagine what is happening. It's Friday night and the end of the week is going to begin. You have arranged a bicycle visit with companions or family for the next day. You have to leave just in time to take advantage of the weather at the start of the day and make the most of the day. When you hit the hay, your heart skips a beat at the thought of getting out into nature again and breathing in the outside air. You anticipate working out, investing energy with individuals you like, talking with them, making a decent stop en route lastly loosening up following a long hard week and leaving your life of all. days a long way behind. You fall asleep with this feeling of expectation and wake up beautifully the next morning, ready to go and inspired. Uplifting goals make you reactive, which quickly prevents you from remembering the last vestiges of weariness. Enjoy your morning espresso, immediately gather your packets, and leave feeling great. The day with each of its companies expects you to take full advantage of them on a consistent basis.

I'm certain you know that inclination. It doesn't make any difference assuming you love bicycle rides, mountain strolls, or exhibition hall visits, in the event that you like to spend your Saturdays in a kayak, on the football field, or work on your nearly completed model airplane: we as a whole prefer to do things that touch off. our energy.

How much simpler everything is the point at which our inward inspiration moves us en route! At the point when we realize we will accomplish something we like, something that brings us happiness. Wouldn't it be amazing if we moved the inspiration of a day like that to the different days of our lives? Assuming we can answer the question "What do I get up at the start of the day for?" without sweating and excellent security, in all sincerity? Wouldn't that be a tantalizing plan to regularly awaken to the awareness of having a task that gives meaning and satisfaction to our lives?

IKIGAI's superb way of thinking shows that it is not necessarily just a vision of paradise. To work on it a bit, iki could be interpreted as "life" and gai implies something like " reason, importance, result, esteem, or worth".

- The significance of life
- What merits living for
- The inclination that it merits getting up toward the beginning of the day
- The favorable luck to do things that make daily routine worth experiencing
- Individual satisfaction and inspiration throughout everyday life
- The sensation of being alive
- The justification for living
- Happiness and an objective throughout everyday life

Ultimately, IKIGAI portrays the perspective of someone who sees reason in everyday life and is therefore lucky enough to have something important to do. The individuals who have perceived their IKIGAI experience bliss throughout everyday life and inward fulfillment, are hopeful, and feel invigorated.

They are propelled and adept at the excitement, have inner strength and extraordinary flexibility. Obviously, they know what they live for and in which direction they should direct their lives. However, IKIGAI does not only allude to the important feeling of satisfaction felt by individuals who know what their life's endowment is.

The term additionally applies to explicit exercises, conditions, associations with others, perspectives or interests, dreams and objectives, and substantially more. In somewhat improved terms, we can say that our own IKIGAI is comprised of four significant topical regions. These are:

- The things we truly prefer to do
- Our assets for sure we are great at
- The things for which we are paid or might be paid for, or for which we might get some sort of remuneration from others
- Things the world requirements

A few components of our IKIGAI have a place just with one region, while others can be put in various classes or even in each of the four. Allow me to disclose this to you utilizing a few explicit models.

For a professional pianist who assigns music as his IKIGAI, each of the four regions assumes a part. The musician does something he enjoys doing. An occupation fills him. Likewise, playing the piano is something he's good at, implying that it's more of one of his strengths. Moreover, since he does not only plays the piano at home for his happiness but also performs in front of an audience, he is working on something for the world.

The people who attend his shows appreciate his music and his virtuoso ability, perhaps, in any case, derive their own IKIGAI from it. In addition, to conclude, the pianist is paid to play and can earn money with it.

He is therefore lucky enough to realize what makes his life beneficial. He can feel his energy, develop his abilities, and constantly have something important to do. It gives him inspiration, happiness, inner fulfillment, and progress towards new goals to pursue. Plus, what he does is quite practical in that he can earn enough to pay the bills.

IKIGAI is not just for people like our pianists who have found incredible enthusiasm in their lives and can make it their calling. It is also contained in smaller and more subtle things in which we mistakenly see little meaning. For example, someone can also observe IKIGAI by constantly watching the sun rise, going for a run with companions, leafing through books to immerse themselves in various worlds, repeating treatments, being there for the family, taking long walks with the dog, learning another unknown dialect, encountering your inventiveness in an artistic creation internship. From the smallest things to exceptionally huge undertakings: the potential results are very different. Additionally, for individuals who have yet to observe their IKIGAI, researching it very well may be exactly that IKIGAI!

What benefit is even more important throughout everyday life assuming we run continuously starting with one setting and then onto the next, checking our messages at regular intervals and letting our cell phone direct our inner speed? With each of the difficulties of a hectic day-to-day life, should we neglect to ensure we have sufficient balance, we will be so worried, tense, or exhausted that we cannot attempt to feel our IKIGAI, let alone set a few parts of it as a regular occurrence.

The important thing is to live cohesively, enjoy free time, and make sure that you have a good overall arrangement with all that is taken into account, on different levels. In this way, we have something to neutralize the pressure and other energy-consuming elements that could weaken us, and we also give space to the best things throughout daily life and our IKIGAI.

Relaxing

Stress and pressure frequently lead to shallow breathing and unfortunate oxygen accessibility. Subsequently, we rapidly feel drained and depleted. Routinely give cognizant consideration to your breathing and attempt to make it a propensity to inhale smoothly and profoundly done in quick-moving circumstances. Contemplation is a decent way to start by intentionally focusing on the breath. When you have something standard, you'll deal with just about any circumstance and get small-scale breathing activity. It has a moment of release from the impact, making you feel revived. Remember - AT DIFFERENT TIMES IN YOUR DAY... How are you breathing right now?

Practice good eating habits

Despite all the different models of wellness, a large number of individuals consume so many calories and too few supplements. Foods are low in fiber and nutrients and often contain excessive amounts of sugar, salt, and a wide range of added substances. This applies specifically to prepared dinners delivered economically.

It is interesting to study the conventional Okinawan diet. It includes heaps of various new foods grown from the ground and soy products like tofu, tons of kelp and fish, and generally little meat. Also, the suppers are very low in fat and salt and low in sugar. The Japanese additionally drink a ton of green tea and have an intriguing standard known as "harahachibu". The idea is to stop eating with your stomach 80% full.

Adequate activity

Ensure you work out regularly. It loosens up us, lessens pressure, and works on our physical and mental execution. Here we can follow the case of Okinawa islanders: they stay dynamic and new into advanced age. It's time to get off that couch!

The rest

- The right rest to confront the days in a fiery manner.
- Balance among work and private life.
- We can for the most part adapt to extraordinary work stages and, surprisingly, over the top pressure for a specific period very well. In any case, when we face difficulties like this, we want to track down a good arrangement eventually.
- Upsetting periods ought to be trailed by extensive stretches of rest and unwinding.

Building strength

Each of the essential elements recorded above helps to develop our flexibility. In the case where we are in psychophysical balance, the problems upset us significantly less than when we are anxious and almost at the restriction of our solidarity. In addition, our IKIGAI also assumes an important part when it comes to flexibility.

In case we consider our lives as important and see it as our moral obligation to structure it as we see fit, it is easier for us to counter hostile external conditions and great chances to maintain an inner air in balance or to recover it quickly. In the words of language teaching originator Viktor Frankl: "Assuming there is one thing that could help individuals through hardships, it is the information on something like an importance."

Living in the Community

Investing energy with others has endless constructive results on us. It advances our comic inclination, our amiability, and our social exercises. New motivations and different assessments help us.

We find many novelties, especially as others guide them to us. A companion might take us to a show or craft show, occasions we might never have considered attending. Many things, like games, are easier if we destroy them. Others give us an unlimited pool of suggestions that we can access at any time. Moreover, stable and reliable connections make us feel like we have a place, which is of great value.

1
WHY CHANGE YOUR LIFE PERSPECTIVE?

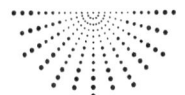

Is it a " Gianni triste " or an "Anna is totally off the mark" in your work or your personal life? You know the type: No matter what, these individuals usually have a negative opinion. They are disappointing and exhausting to the people around them, on the grounds that their pessimism drains the pleasure of everything. Assuming Anna goes bad, she gets an honor at work, for example, she complains that her administrator's celebratory speech was exhausting or she ruled out some niceties. Also, if Gianni triste is lucky enough to win this contest, the main remark that escapes his mouth would likely be a protest at the expense he would have to pay for his multimillion-dollar prize.

Certain individuals appear to not be able to quit being negative. Be that as it may, stop and think for a minute: they're settling on a decision to get it done. As deals legend, Tom Hopkins put it, "Being despondent is a propensity. The decision is yours."

Deploy an improvement for your well-being by changing your point of view. Try not to underestimate the power of positive reasoning! For a certain something, it can influence your wellbeing. Specialists from Johns Hopkins University have observed that an uplifting perspective can add to the fight against coronary heart disease. A review (part of the large Nurses' Health Study, which began in 1976) by analysts at Harvard University and Brigham and Women's Hospital found comparable results: We observed a solid and genuinely critical relationship of expanding levels of good faith with diminishing mortality gambles, including mortality from every one of the significant reasons for death, like a malignant growth, coronary illness, stroke, respiratory sickness, and contamination.

There are many valid justifications for being a positive brain. So why are these countless individuals caught up in bad reasoning? How could they have arrived?

BEGINNINGS OF NEGATIVE REASONING

A pessimistic view frequently comes from feeling disgraceful, maybe because of being scrutinized or embarrassed by guardians, educators, companions, or other persuasive individuals in somebody's day-to-day existence. In the long run, this individual disguises these pessimistic remarks and eventually makes them their own: external pessimistic remarks coordinated to this individual become negative self-talk, giving truth to the well-known statement "You are the cause of all your own problems".

How might you change those restricting convictions? How might you recapture your ability to think emphatically? Venture out towards change, have a significant impact on your viewpoint. Rather than thinking, "What is the point of being positive? Nothing is ever really great for me in any case," stop in your strides and pose yourself this inquiry, "Is this valid? Have I never lived it up?"

Last week you completed a business on time and a financial plan! On your last getaway, you figured out how to take a nice shot that was in the center and didn't have a focal point-darkening thumb! Last month you saw a movie that you enjoyed! Earlier in the day, the toast you had for breakfast was just awesome!

Whenever you continue to understand that line of reasoning, you will track down a wide range of cheerful occasions and accomplishments in your day-to-day existence, numerous positive encounters. Extend your reasoning to challenge the presumption that cynicism should be prevailing. Then, at that point, you will comprehend that cynicism isn't like "things are consistently for me" and that you don't need to acknowledge it as the state of affairs. The following are nine hints to work on your viewpoint.

1. **Begin with a decent night's rest**

Rehearsing great rest cleanliness makes you awaken with a more splendid perspective on the day, keeps you sound, and works on your efficiency.

1. **Reserve some time for yourself**

You cannot constantly take advantage of others and their demands. Where could you be? Can we say that you deal with yourself, do you consider yourself? Do you do things that you enjoy or that satisfy you?

1. **Remain associated**

Being important to an informal organization gives the feeling of having a place. Close and personal associations, for example, participating, joining a church or local gatherings, or meeting a companion help to diminish feelings of abandonment and segregation.

1. **Move**

Dynamic activity can work on your mindset and perspective. Assuming you can, go for a walk or swim. Swing golf clubs. Do each of the exercises that you enjoy and that gets you moving.

1. **Rethink your day**

I asked my kids what their day was like when they got home from school. In any case, I saw that they regularly told me negative things about their day. Currently, I ask them, "What was the most awesome aspect of your day?" This compels them to search out the features of their day that were recently ignored. The more we search for positive angles in our day-to-day existence, the more we find!

1. **Keep in mind, cash purchases things, not bliss**

Contemplate your needs, your qualities. Do useful things that make you more extravagant and that additionally has a social worth.

1. **Practice pardoning**

While we stick to harshness and hatred, we just hurt ourselves. We don't reject that we have been harmed and outraged, yet we conclude that we never again need to be limited by them. Absolution liberates us.

1. **Provide for other people**

It's been experimentally shown that when we give, our brain's reward circuitry is activated, causing happier and more fulfilled feelings. Studies have further shown that charitable practices are linked to our ability to experience good feelings. Thereafter, giving is related to bliss.

1. **Keep in mind, you don't need to do it impeccably**

Rather than focusing on bombarding goals, focus on that big, deeper inclination for change. Extraordinary annual insurance is like a fresh start. Yet give yourself the ease of starting over each day.

2
SIMPLIFY

You've probably heard words like cleaning, rearranging, simple living, etc. thrown around many times. Either way, you might be wondering what he intends to make your life easier? "Improve on your life" is vague, since it can mean various things to various individuals.

Maybe you are planning to clean your house making your life easier. Either way, another person might believe that improving your life means being more in tune with how you invest your energy. What's more, here's the critical step. Nor is off-base! These are the two methods for making your life more straightforward.

Working on your life can include various viewpoints and activities. What's more, one of those terms can truly mean anything you desire it to mean. Anything definition assists you with concluding what's significant in your life and what's simply adding mess and interruption.

Work on Your Life, what Does It Mean?

Whenever I consider making your life simpler, I consider it any activity or change you make to remove interruptions from your home and your life. Essentially, eliminate clutter from your life.

However, in addition to the actual things that add mess to your home. Furthermore, the things that add mental mess, passion endlessly mess to your timetable. Also, the motivation behind why eliminating these interruptions is so significant is on the grounds that it permits you to zero in additional on the things you worth and matter most to you. Count the actual things you own, your associations with loved ones, how much time you want to spend on the exercises you enjoy, from there the sky is the limit. Working on your life involves eliminating interruptions to make it happen in your home and in your life to focus on what makes the biggest difference to you.

Two sections to make your life simpler. To remove the interruptions, I like to consider disentangling in two sections. The initial segment is eliminating the actual mess from your home. The things that are taking your time, space, and energy, without enhancing your life.

Furthermore, the subsequent part is eliminating the messiness from your time and timetable. Pointless action that is depleting you, however, doesn't enhance your life, isn't great for you, or perhaps hurts you.

FOCUS ON WHAT MAKES THE BIGGEST DIFFERENCE TO YOU

Working on your life involves shedding the layers of clutter, overabundance, interruptions, and exercise so you can see what makes the biggest difference for you. And then make sure that how you use your time, space, and energy is in line with what makes the biggest difference to you and what you value the most.

There's a great statement from Annie Dillard that summarizes it impeccably. According to him, "The manner in which we spend our days is, obviously, the manner in which we spend our lives." It is how you live consistently that determines how you go on with your life. Also, who needs to look back on his life and recognize that he spent his days overseeing the mess, busy with unnecessary responsibilities and worried?

CAN WE SAY THAT YOU ARE TRAPPED IN AN ECONOMIC CYCLE?

The moment you're bothered by clutter, interruptions, and hype, those aren't entirely obvious needs. Or on the other hand, at any rate, you find yourself sidetracked by this because you are busy trying to stay on top of the daily schedule.

It's almost similar to the fact that you're so caught up in the do, a pattern that it's not hard not to remember why you're doing it! Your days become a frantic pace to track, gather, tidy, arrive, arrive, etc. Additionally, you end up depriving yourself of chances to associate with loved ones, participate in your home instead of following along, and carry along with a daily existence that feels good instead of allowing it to be consummated.

Work on your life to escape a pattern of responsibilities and interruptions. In any case, fortunately, there is an exit from that sort of cycle. At the point when you improve on your life, you deliberately find ways to eliminate the messiness, overabundance, free-for, and superfluous interruptions from your life. Give yourself the time, space, and energy you need to focus on your needs, your qualities.

IMPROVE ON YOUR LIFE

It begins with the actual issue. While you're finding a way ways to make your life simpler, it's regularly more straightforward to begin by eliminating the actual mess and interruptions from your home. Eliminating actual mess implies acting with substantial articles that you can see, gather and simply decide.

Cleaning up your home takes some psychological work. Step by step instructions to make progress with propensities and examples. Work on relinquishing the connections you might hold.

Furthermore, figure out how to see the value in the space you are making. However, in numerous ways dispensing with the actual mess from your house is simpler than cleaning the messiness off of your head, the psychological mess you've been hefting around for quite a long time, or old restricting propensities and convictions. Taking out actual mess shows you the abilities you can expand on

An awesome symptom of wiping out the actual mess from your home initially is that the more mess you eliminate, the less time and energy your home takes for this request to be kept up with, giving you additional time and energy to chip away at eliminating wellsprings of mental mess.

It likewise gives you apparent and quick outcomes that show you the advantages of rearrangements. At the point when you clear the messiness, your home goes from overpowering and turbulent to easier and more serene. Furthermore, it quickly shows you the force of disentanglement.

Clearing your home of real clutter is also an incredible chance to work on improving recognition and letting go of the things that add clutter to your life and don't give enough value as a compromise. Then, at that point, you can utilize those abilities and encounters to recognize and relinquish what isn't serving you well and take out theoretical mess and interruptions.

WORK ON YOUR LIFE, TIME, AND SCHEDULES

With real space altogether, now is a good time to direct your focus to general rearrangements. Begin searching for immaterial spots where mess and interruptions can stow away.

Places like your schedule with an excessive amount to do and not sufficient opportunity to do everything and safeguard your mental soundness. Or then again the perpetual mental plan for the day that you generally heft around with you. Or then again even the regions in your day-to-day existence where you generally feel two stages behind and never feel totally in charge.

BEGIN BY RECOGNIZING THE AREAS OF STRESS

Recognize this immaterial wreck by asking yourself what's adding the most pressure to your life at present? Is it the dinner arrangement? Such a large number of commitments that cause you to feel depleted? Staying aware of Household Chores? Do you wish to have more opportunities to enjoy yourself with your kids, and so on? You can't fix it if you don't have the foggiest idea of what should be fixed. What's going on with your life now?

Likewise, notice what's working in the meantime. What satisfies you, fills your cup, assists you with feeling in charge of your time and days, and so on?

Search for normal subjects or moves you have made that make these parts of your all-consuming purpose for you. Consider it a daily existence review. Recognize what works, what doesn't. What is it that you want? Where you're going wrong? Then, at that point, make a move and change what doesn't work.

It is a sluggish excursion. It's extremely normal a sluggish course of experimentation, attempting various things to see what works best in your life. See what's right now occupying your time and schedule. Is it true or not that you are ready to change or eliminate responsibilities, exercises, or commitments that add more pressure to your life than esteem?

Are there any new propensities, schedules, or rhythms you can attempt to assist your days with moving along as expected? How might you lessen the things that cause you stress, interruption, and mental issue?

Keep in mind that this can incorporate incredible sources of stress and interruption, such as excessively upsetting work. Or on the other hand little wellsprings of interruption, for example, things that take time when it very well may be spent in better ways assuming you adjust yourself more to your qualities. For instance, taking a gander at how much time spent via web-based media or on the telephone, when you need to have additional time.

The goal is to give you more time, space, opportunity, and harmony to meet the one you fulfill the most. Whenever you have fewer things that add confusion and disruption to your life, you have more energy for what you value and for your needs. Expanding your home and your schedule allows you to be more aware of what fills your home and your days.

Rearranging, eliminating mess, and interruptions liberate you, placing you in charge of what occupies your time, space, and timetable, hauling you out of the pattern of basic endurance, and offering you the chance to begin flourishing.

Lastly, when you feel less depleted, less pushed, have additional time, and feel more in charge of where your time goes, you have the chance to reside all the more calmly. You purposefully pick what fills your home and your days to make it work for you, and figure out how to see the value in the space you are making.

3
THE BENEFITS OF MEDITATION

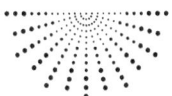

The benefits are diverse and extensive; in fact, contemplation is practically like a "happiness pill" that any of us can take, and it costs nothing. The best part is that it's easier than you naturally think. It can very well be done anywhere; reflection does not need proper design. You can do this while walking the dog, while you brush with your pony, standing on a seat. There is no wrong way to think, as long as there is your true expectation.

If you haven't put aside the opportunity to think about it lately, here are 23 reasons to put it back on your list of needs.

1. You will rest better. Restless, cheer! Contemplation of care further develops an individual's quality of rest, especially in the elderly.
2. You will bring down your pulse. Studies have demonstrated that care reflection, which assists you with relinquishing repressed strain, is a characteristic method for bringing down the pulse. Certain individuals even trait

their everyday contemplation discipline to the capacity to lessen their dependence on circulatory strain drugs.

3. Contemplation assists you with overseeing unpleasant circumstances better. At the point when you can venture into a tranquil, careful space consistently, you can feel quieter generally speaking and will direct your feelings and better deal with the day-to-day stressors that could regularly drive you past the brink.
4. Contemplation diminishes misery and worry. Mark Ruffalo is a VIP who explained how reflection "saved" him from jitters. In any case, countless others suffering from misery and fears are also feeling the benefits. The country's malignant growth communities also provide spaces for patient reflection. Preparing our contemplations to focus on "right now" rather than apprehensions is so helpful in any case when you are going through a difficult time. Moreover, indeed, I also know this by direct insight!
5. Contemplation soothes torments. Inconceivable but Obvious: Studies have shown that reflection can sometimes replace opiates for patients suffering from ongoing torment. Although not a solution, as victims of torment will tell you, even a little help can be important. Many have found the reflection important to release the physical and passionate aggravation of treating malignant breast growth.
6. You will help your invulnerable frame. A new UCLA investigation has found that thoughtful HIV patients can "slow down" the breakdown of their CD-4 cells (these are the resistant cells that are assaulted and wiped out by the infection).
7. You will feel the good consequences of reflection in minutes. It's validated! Many investigations have been shown that you will feel the advantages of reflection in the

blink of an eye. And keeping in mind that consistently counts, to come by the best outcomes, practice it for no less than 25 minutes per day for three back-to-back days, as per Carnegie Mellon University.

8. Reflection makes an individual more sympathetic. Science confirms it. The sympathy and benevolence we feel as a result of interfacing with our internal identities through contemplation extend not only to other people but also to creatures.
9. The "seemingly insignificant details" won't irritate you like they typically do. You will be more mindful. Subsequently, you will feel better ready to confront your day calmly when little stressors emerge.
10. Individuals who reflect are more joyful. Satisfaction is something we all strive for, right? The reflection takes us there, in fact, focuses on the spectacle that you are actually "reworking your mind" for joy. Science says there are seven propensities we can repeat for a happier life. Prepare to have your mind blown. Contemplation will take care of everything!
11. Contemplation helps improve memory and the ability to concentrate and learn. Students who participated in "care preparation" preferentially performed the GRE over those who did not. Also, remember, children, are never too young to even think about learning to think (and experience its beneficial results!).
12. The general nature of your life will improve. Notwithstanding all the logically demonstrated medical advantages of contemplation, you will start to feel greater satisfaction in your day-to-day routine.
13. You will feel calmer during the day. You will be more adjusted.
14. You will work more efficiently. Contemplation is the

mystery of success for CEOs and well-known artists. Indeed, even organizations like Google and Apple are urging their employees to think twice, considering how this contributes to the benefits. That's why everyone at Google is thinking.

15. It can help you quit smoking and other addictive practices.
16. Reflection can lessen the gamble of respiratory failure. Contemplation helps you reduce the pressure you feel throughout daily life, which can help you fight cardiovascular disease.
17. A few scientists accept that contemplation might even safeguard against Alzheimer's and dementia.
18. Oversees torment. While managing anguish and misfortune, it can seem like nothing can at any point help. Be that as it may, when you ponder, you are preparing your psyche away from the injuries of yesterday and the apprehensions of tomorrow.
19. Reflection assists you with managing the awful accidents of your past. Comparable to n. 18 above, veterans and those experiencing PTSD have tracked down a great deal of help in contemplation.
20. It will help you to be available and to live in that moment. How many of us are constantly running? However, at that point, we wonder where the day went and want to go back. Part of pursuing a mindful daily routine is experiencing (and drawing a charge from) the second as we experience it. Reflection can help you embrace more of those minutes.

1. You will acquire a superior comprehension of your more profound self. Furthermore, contemplation can assist reinforce your association with your instinct.

2. Contemplation can help you feel enlivened in new ways. Do you need to do some conceptualization? Is there a problem to solve? Focusing your brain on thinking can help you see things in new and varied ways.
3. In a real sense, it reshapes your brain. Each of the positive views recorded above stems from the physiological impacts of contemplation on the real mind.

4
ZEN MEDITATION

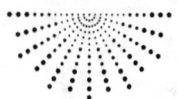

What is Zen? It is both something we are, our real essence articulated in second-to-second thoughts, and something we do, a restricted practice through which we can understand the pleasure of being. It is anything but a framework of conviction that is made proselytes. There is no authoritative opinion or regulation. Harmony is the immediate experience of what could be called a definitive reality, or the pure and simple, but it is not independent of the conventional, of the member of the family. This immediate experience is our heritage. The act of zazen, reflection, is a method for understanding the non-dualistic, energetic, unassuming and interconnected nature of all life.

It is this path of recognition that was shown about 2500 years ago by the Indian ruler Siddhartha Gautama, who became known as Buddha Shakyamuni. "Buddha" basically means "one who is restless". His incredible instruction was that we can all move; that we are essentially Buddhas: Jewish Buddhas, Christian Buddhas, Hindu Buddhas, Islamic Buddhas, Ashanti Buddhas, Haudenosaunee Buddhas, and Traditional Buddhas.

With this adaptable and obliging mentality towards the different societies and convictions it experienced, Buddhism was embraced all through Asia. In China, it converged with Taoism and advanced into Ch'an, the Chinese word for reflection, which became "Harmony" in Japan. In late many years it has turned into a fundamental piece of Western culture. To be sure, antiquarian Arnold Toynbee has contended that one of the main occasions of the 20th century was the development of Buddhism from East to West.

Through devoted and steady reflection practice, we can understand that the other and oneself are One, that the fashioned and the unconditioned are synchronous, that the pure and the relative are indistinguishable. From this recognition comes steady empathy and insight, a calm and naturally appropriate reaction to any conditions that may emerge. We don't dwell on it too much; we don't call it religion. Whenever the Dalai Lama received information about Buddhism, he said, "My religion is thoughtfulness."

All in all, once again, what is Zen? Stop now. Stop trying to get a scientific lock on something huge and limitless, undeniably beyond what the savvy brain can master. Be mindful. Enjoy the breath. I completely like that. Exhale now, gradually, with equal appreciation. Allow it all to go, go all out. exhale with affection. Obtaining and Offering: Doing it with care and consistency is the revolutionary practice we call Zen.

This basic yet meaningful practice can free us from the shackles of the past and the future, as well as the willful and restraining obstructions we erect around what we mistakenly think are our different and permanent selves.

Who do we suppose we are, at any rate? At the point when we truly look profoundly, it turns into the "Who am I?" We observe that the adapted perspectives and habitual characteristics we call "self" have no proper substance. We can, through reliable zazen, free ourselves from that sham self and find the genuine self, the being that is open, sure, and unhindered, streaming with all that exists at present. So normally we deal with the climate, beginning with our activities: not squandering the valuable assets of the earth, understanding that each act has results. Also, normally enough we broaden this Mind; we vow to live with care, trustworthiness, and genuineness; we commit to liberating all creatures from torment.

Harmony reflection is an antiquated Buddhist practice that traces back to the Tang line in the seventh century in China. From its Chinese origin, it has spread to Korea, Japan, and other Asian terrains where it keeps on flourishing. The Japanese expression "Harmony" is a subsidiary of the Chinese word Ch'an, itself an interpretation of the Indian expression dhyana, and that implies fixation or reflection.

Harmony reflection is a conventional Buddhist discipline that can be drilled by both new and experienced meditators. Similarly, as with different types of Buddhist contemplation, Zen practice can help individuals in a heap of ways, including furnishing devices to assist in adapting to melancholy and nervousness issues. The more deeply object is otherworldly, as the act of Zen reflection uncovers the inborn clearness and usefulness of the brain. In Zen, to encounter this unique nature of the psyche is to encounter arousing.

Harmony resolves well-established questions and general inquiries of life that regularly appear to need replies, and it does as such based on training and instinct instead of contemplating and rationale. Harmony/Ch'an has been broadly depicted by the incomparable Buddhist expert Bodhidharma as "An exceptional transmission outside the lessons; not laid out on words and letters;

pointing straightforwardly to the human brain; seeing nature and turning into a Buddha".

All schools of Zen work on seated reflection called Zazen, where one sits upright and follows the breath, particularly the development of the breath within the body. Some Zen schools also practice koans, a kind of deep enigma that is presented by an expert in Zen contemplation to the understudy, to help him overcome his judicious constraints to bear witness to the truth beyond weighing. A popular koan is "The thing is a clapping hand?" Traditionally, this training requires a constant association between a true Zen ace and a truly dedicated understudy. Rather than offering brief arrangements, it resolves the major issues. The training focuses on the genuine reason for the despondency and disappointment we have all accomplished and moves our consideration such that prompts genuine agreement.

The genuine key to joy isn't riches or acclaim, it is inside us. Like any remaining certified otherworldly ways, Buddhism instructs that the more you provide for other people, the more you procure. It additionally supports mindfulness and enthusiasm for things throughout everyday life.

CONTEMPLATION PROCEDURES

Breath perception

Meditators ought to expect an agreeable stance, for example, the Burmese, Half Lotus, or Seiza present during zazen. Mindfulness is coordinated towards a specific object of contemplation, normally the perception of the breath. This technique cultivates a consistent feeling of presence and carefulness.

Calm mindfulness

Here, meditators figure out how to permit contemplations to course through their brains without judgment, connection, or dismissal. The Japanese call this training shikantaza, or "simply sitting". This Zen Buddhist contemplation method is drilled without a reflection article, anchors, or substance. The lessons emphasize that there is no goal, essentially. The meditator "collapses" and allows their psyche to be. Zazen is not a necessary evil: it is the end.

Serious gathering reflection

Genuine meditators consistently practice thorough gathering reflection in contemplation communities or sanctuaries. The Japanese call this training sesshin. Experts give the vast majority of their chance to sit a reflection. Every meeting goes on around 30-50 minutes, rotating with reflection, strolling, brief breaks, and suppers. Dinners are eaten peacefully. Indeed, even brief times of work are done deliberately. Today such Zen contemplation withdraws are polished in Taiwan, Japan, and the West.

5
WHAT IS IKIGAI

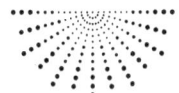

Suicide is the incredible vacancy or meaninglessness throughout daily life. I've heard it myself many times, trying to think things through and find a way.

COULD YOU UNDERSTAND IKIGAI?

There are endless speculations connected with IKIGAI, we can't characterize a solitary or right idea about the word, various creators and analysts share various thoughts regarding these ideas that connect with the reason for life.

The mystery of individuals of Okinawa and other Japanese regions lies in light food, satisfactory rest, and exercise. Somewhat they are right, however, it likewise requires the individual to have euphoria throughout everyday life, something that prompts him to experience consistently.

Running against the norm, even those searching for the distinction and cash that can make dreams materialize, end up vacant and random, without arriving at the genuine bliss that can be caught and concealed inside us.

You want to escape the groove, off autopilot, or innumerable tedious days. Pause and inquire as to whether you are fulfilled. Also, don't be tricked into thinking there are no other options or arrangements. Attempt to venture out behind your fantasies and never surrender! We shouldn't contrast ourselves with others or wish for the very satisfaction that others "apparently" have. We need to zero in on ourselves we need to run at our speed.

Simply adoring doing something isn't to the point of discovering that we will be fruitful and talented at it. We should acknowledge our impediments and spotlight our capacities as opposed to attempting to foster inconceivable abilities, yet try constantly!

IKIGAI is something individual that no one but you can comprehend. So commit yourself to investigate your brain. Today we just pursue directions and live in a group impact. Without our viewpoints, we are worried, and we disdain and grumble. And keeping in mind that we enjoy childish delights, we neglect to track down satisfaction, worth, and reason. We should all have our specific manner of reasoning and acting, regarding that of others. The battle is day to day and not fooling around with individuals who are negative or who don't assist us with accomplishing our objective.

The world requires positive outcomes, our activities influence individuals around us, causing the fiasco that is our nation and the world overall. Assuming you apply at minimum a portion of IKIGAI's thoughts, you will track down the genuine significance of life, as well as accomplish your fantasies and objectives.

Such changes plan to make you more joyful, better, have a prosperous existence with how much cash you need, have a long and full life. IKIGAI can make you live longer, be better, be less worried, or more all it assists you with having an objective and a justification behind living.

Whenever you concentrate on IKIGAI you will see that dietary patterns, notable activities, and different exercises are firmly connected with IKIGAI. Without these practices, you basically can not accomplish the satisfying life reason that you are searching for. IKIGAI is a Japanese word that signifies "justification for being". All in all, IKIGAI gets you up consistently. To observe your IKIGAI, you want to begin with something basic, the entire way to the major objectives.

6
THE FIVE PILLARS OF IKIGAI TO RECONNECT WITH YOURSELF

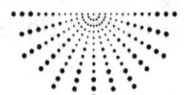

*K*odawari is the Japanese word that alludes to the blend of fastidious meticulousness in what the future held unrivaled delight we feel in what the future held. Kodawari is a basic piece of IKIGAI (elocution), "a Japanese word to portray the delights and implications of life. The word in a real sense comprises iki (to live) and gai (reason)." Therefore, it is inexactly deciphered as your justification behind living or why you awaken consistently.

Writer and neuroscientist Ken Mogi, in his book Awakening Your IKIGAI, states that IKIGAI "is utilized in different settings and can be applied to little ordinary things as well as to major objectives and results. Above all, IKIGAI is conceivable without fundamentally having an outcome in your expert life... doubtlessly having IKIGAI can prompt achievement, yet achievement is certainly not a vital condition for having IKIGAI. It is available to every one of us ". To this end, Mogi presents the five mainstays of IKIGAI which he accepts exemplify this idea and assist us with taking advantage of each second.

Point of support 1: Start Small → Focus on the subtleties.

Point of support 2: Free yourself → Accept what your identity is.

Point of support 3: Harmony and maintainability → Trust in others.

Point of support 4: The delight of seemingly insignificant details → Appreciate tactile joy.

Point of support 5: Being in the present time and place → Finding your stream.

Mogi calls attention to that the support points are commonly building up and permit IKIGAI to flourish, yet they are not "totally unrelated or far-reaching, nor do they have a specific request or order."

IKIGAI is firmly connected with our feeling of satisfaction. And keeping in mind that Mogi states that there is no outright equation for bliss, she expresses that being tolerant yourself is "a low-spending plan, support free recipe for being cheerful. Accepting yourself is one of the least demanding, easiest and most remunerating things you could do. for yourself ".

Nonetheless, Mogi recognizes that no man is an island and draws a relationship: "A man resembles a woodland, individual however associated and reliant upon others for development." And as well as gaining and getting support from others, perhaps the quickest method for developing is to gain from disappointment. "All things considered, in the long course of life, once in a while you stagger and fall. Indeed, even in those minutes, you can have IKIGAI, in any event, when you are in a losing streak".

"IKIGAI, more or less, is in a real sense from support to grave, whatever occurs in your life." IKIGAI implies staying alert and present, partaking in the easily overlooked details that make up the second we are living in, and observing our stream as we become mixed up in liking the subtleties. Also, when something turns out badly, "as long as you have IKIGAI, you can get by in troublesome times in your day-to-day existence. You can generally return to your place of refuge, where you can begin the experiences of your life once more ".

ACTIVITY

Today: Take a gander at the five mainstays of IKIGAI. What number do you apply to your life? What number of could do you profit from the application? Make the goal to know and be mindful of every one of the 5 support points and apply them no less than once today.

Future: Celebrate your identity and your IKIGAI! Additionally, start repeating healing and monitoring the five pillars of IKIGAI, with the goal of being able to apply them to as many events in your daily existence as possible.

7
FLOW

*I*kigai hails from Okinawa, Japan's most seasoned local area, both as far as local area establishment and the normal life expectancy of its residents. Their whole local area, where satisfying 110 is the thing to take care of, is revolved around this rule, which Okinawans allude to as "why we get up toward the beginning of the day."

The center of IKIGAI is the crossing point of what you love (enthusiasm), what you are great at (calling), what the world (or clients, for this situation) needs (mission), and what you can get compensated for (employment).

There are a few fundamental standards of this way of thinking, however, a major piece of IKIGAI is getting to those minutes every day when you are getting things done with preeminent concentration and satisfaction (you might realize that you are in the zone or track down your stream). The following are three demonstrated strategies for organizing your chance to assist you with tracking down your stream.

BE WHERE YOU ARE AND LIVE IN THAT TIME

This is the center rule of IKIGAI. To be the place where you are and live in that time, you want to figure out how to wipe out interruptions. All things considered, how could you enter a flow condition and stay there amidst the constant bustle of messages, instant messages, and warnings of successive chats and gatherings?

It takes about 15 minutes of continuous concentration to accomplish a transition condition. Following interference, however, it may take more than 25 minutes to refocus. By the time you have 10 continuous gatherings on a lonely day, you may feel like you're late before your day even begins. In addition, it can prompt to perform various tasks at gatherings.

Whenever you perform various tasks, your mind can't process or store data as well as when you center around each errand in turn. Individuals reduce their utility by 60% and lower their IQ by more than 10 points when multitasking. I turned off Outlook warnings and inner conversation step notices and silenced the phone. I focus on checking for warnings three times a day where I go through and respond to messages and calls.

I admit I felt a little uncomfortable from the start. I was so used to multitasking and jumping from call to call that I felt a little remorseful like I needed to accomplish more than whatever I was currently focusing on. As we eat, our reliable phone informs us that another email has recently appeared in our inbox. We are basically generally associated now. So how could it work to not be so deeply responsive (and again, less busy)? Deliciously, in fact. Everything I focus on stands out enough to be noticed. I'm not behind on any work and I have an incredible eye for respecting others by being 100% there for them. By reserving the time of my day to build flow, I'm better at my specific job, better at responding, and less focused.

Increment your flow, but also test yourself with your abilities. Whenever you know what brings you into your flow, it's essential to extend that time, while challenging yourself in that range of abilities.

If you're a developer, learn how to use another programming language. Assuming you are a venture capital administrator, recognize and acquire skills with a different job arrangement than executive abilities. Look for ways to test yourself so you don't find yourself burnt out and stuck doing the same thing you're doing now 10-15 years from now.

Gradually, I get a lot of happiness from being sorted (indeed, I'm a geek like that) and working with technological devices. Work in continuous time so that I do these things with a preeminent fixation. In Mihaly Csikszentmihalyi's book "Stream - Psychology of bliss". Yuval describes the gigantic progress we have made in all areas (specialist, clinical, social, and monetary), but he notes that we have barely advanced on the stepping stone of human joy.

Mihaly's review shows what it takes to keep us people happy. Use the phrase "stream" to describe how individuals feel when they are completely drawn in or in the "zone" with what they are doing. Individuals are immersed to the point that time seems to no longer exist, they neglect to eat, drink, and even rest. Mihaly describes the important circumstances for individuals to enter the stream and thereby joy. It also shows that satisfaction can be achieved through the current, regardless of external conditions. Individuals need to see an unmistakable objective and know about the directions or rules on the most proficient method to approach accomplishing the objective. Second, they should see that they have the fitting expertise to complete the guidelines or rules, as well as get quick criticism on their advancement towards the objective. Third, individuals should have the option to endlessly zero in on the execution and the criticism they get while performing.

I couldn't resist the opportunity to see the comparability between this "Human Flow" and the "Specialized Flow" wording utilized in Lean. The specialized stream or a continuous "progression of significant worth" is what one plans to accomplish in a Lean association. The specialized stream likewise requires characterized objectives. It requires "standard positions" or interaction rules, as well as a certified group to run after the future state.

Specialized stream, Human stream, what different streams would we say we are mindful of? All things considered, there is the indispensable "Income" that each organization, regardless of how huge or little, should be mindful of. Also, significantly more famous is the steadily developing "Data Flow".

Is it conceivable to incorporate these four streams: Cash, Technical, Information, and Human into a solitary model? Why not check it out? I think income is the mainstream. Numerous Toyota stories return to the possibility that without Cash Flow you can't be answerable for your predetermination. Income is like oxygen, in itself, it has no significance, however, it gives the resources to get all the other things.

The following stream is the specialized stream. Lean gives a large number of the standards on the most proficient method to layout and executes the course through an association's different worth streams. An association, a complex versatile framework ordinarily, has sources of info and results and adheres to basic guidelines or calculations between its singular specialists. These free specialists inside a complex versatile framework are human or non-human commonly.

All in all, certain sources of data and certain results circulate from one machine to another, from one human to another, from human to machine, or from machine to human. These progressions of data sources and results between specialists include the progression of data, which depends on the principles of the specialized flow, essentially the standards of the particular turn of the area being played. In Lean, for example, Kaban is a data flow situation that references the perfect data at the perfect time in the right quality and quantity. The Lean "visual administration" framework is also essential for the flow of information. The visual administration, similar to a dashboard in a game, gives feedback on progress towards a goal or changes that warn us of a potential flutter away from that goal. An Andon is another vital entry sign of the data stream. In summary, the data progression establishes the connection or the correspondence channel between the specialized flow and the human flow.

Human Flow, given Mihaly's exploration, makes us more joyful. To obtain the human flow, the accompanying circumstances must be fulfilled, as they have been examined. Individuals must know what to do, the goal, and how to accomplish it, using the principles while having the appropriate ability. These circumstances are given by the technical flow or the Lean framework. The progress data gives the proper critique expected to perceive how you are progressing towards the goal.

The third condition is the ability to concentrate on the work at hand. I first struggled with this seemingly clear condition. Currently, I think this is the vital rationale for the idea of wastefulness or "Muda" in Toyota's theory. Squander slows down the flow. Waste distracts us from our ability to think. The reference meaning of the word "concentrate" is a "substance obtained by eliminating or diminishing the impairment specialist; a concentrated type of something". In Lean, this simply compares to "added esteem", no unnecessary materials, labor, transportation, etc. Ultimately, we eliminate waste from our executives so we can fully focus on the job at hand – the mission that leads directly to the ideal goal without diversions.

Ozgene's vision "to propel humankind" can subsequently be interpreted "to increment bliss" in view of Mihaly's idea of the human stream. Ozgene's vision of "move interest" portrays the individual assessing whether challenge and saw ability are enough adjusted. On the off chance that the equilibrium is correct, an individual will become inquisitive. Assuming that the objective is set at a significant level, more preparation is required or the individual will become restless. Assuming the test is excessively low for the given expertise level, the individual will rapidly get exhausted and need a higher test.

The reason for the Lean framework, the Technical Flow, is in this manner to permit people to enter the Human Flow and accordingly more joyful staff. The result of the specialized stream satisfies clients by limiting lead times, seeking after zero imperfections, and limiting expenses. Fulfilled clients balance out the income. Thus the idealistic circle keeps on streaming.

Does this specialized stream and satisfaction appear to be excessively far-brought? Watch individuals playing computer games on their cell phones. Clear goals, clear standards, contributing to the moment, absolute focus they forget about time and for the second they're in the zone and feeling joyful.

8
COVERING YOUR REASON FOR BEING

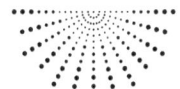

*I*KIGAI is a Japanese idea that implies "motivation to be". The thing wakes you up in the first part of the day. We have IKIGAI overall, however, it is difficult to track it down. IKIGAI is certainly an alluring thought. It's a good idea that this resonates with individuals all over the planet who, like me, are gradually striving to accomplish more happiness, purpose, and validity in their lives.

Here are, without a specific request, 3 surprisingly simple ways that can help you find your purpose:

1. Assuming you could get up tomorrow with one superpower, what could it be?

I'll begin with a pleasant one. I posed this inquiry to a dear companion of mine, Sandy, as of late. A committed and effective correspondence proficient, he is presently head of advertising at a hyper-developing tech startup. He contemplated it cautiously and answered: "Having the option to speak with anybody all over the planet without hindrances."

Isolated from her day job in advertising, Sandy is also a skilled muralist and artist. Plus, the craft business he started with his accomplice has started to take off lately. It would seem that on nights and weekends, Sandy now encounters her superpower. Her wonderful art crosses language barriers and allows her to interact with individuals from all over the world.

1. What will you lament most on your deathbed?
2. What gets you rolling?

9
ACHIEVING IKIGAI

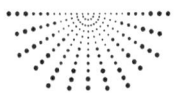

To arrive at our IKIGAI you want a basic fixing: our capacity to enter that stream, which will give us the "ideal experience". IKIGAI is a way of life, in addition to an extended eating regimen that does something amazing.

It expects that you think emphatically, perform well inside your local area, practice good eating habits, and work out consistently. In any case, there is no single sort of activity to keep the brain solid constantly. Jujitsu, for example, is an extremely unlimited Chinese military skill in Japan and on the planet. The equivalent goes for yoga from Indian classes.

Helping others, putting one's desire under the necessities of others, repeating leisure activities, and investing free energy with old friends are fundamental elements of IKIGAI that influence the nature of your life. For instance, distributed research results from Kenji Iida, Senior Visiting Researcher at the KeioResearch Institute at SFC, and Yuko Oguma, Associate Professor at Keio University's Sports Medicine Research Center, showed that the more extended the yoga experience. , the more noteworthy the stream insight.

Furthermore, the Journal of Epidemiology distributed the aftereffects of a concentrate by KimikoTomioka, Norio Kurumatani, Hiroshi Hosoi, subsidiary with Nara Prefectural Health Research Center at Nara Medical University, where they found that not just having leisure activities and a reason in life can delay life span, yet in addition a solid everyday routine hope among the old experiencing locally.

7 IS THE ENCHANTED NUMBER

The seven recently referenced conditions that you should meet to enter the IKIGAI stream presented by specialist Owen Schaffer are as per the following:

1. Know what to do
2. Ability
3. Realizing how well you are doing
4. Know where to go
5. Lay out aggressive difficulties
6. Utilize our gifts
7. No interruptions in our interaction

As may be obvious, getting into the progression of your IKIGAI is easy to talk about, not so easy to do. While certainly feasible, it requires its discipline. Assuming the initial six stages address individual activities, the outcome relies fundamentally upon us, we can't say something very similar for the seventh.

Not being occupied in the time of innovation is a troublesome undertaking. Whenever email, Facebook, Twitter, Instagram, Pinterest notices are quickly springing up on our workstations and telephones, the best way to escape is to make our own private space. Yet, how is it that we could get it? Whenever you have laid out certain propensities, it will be simpler to lose all sense of direction in work.

DID I SAY SEVEN IS WIZARDRY?

So from now on, before you start composing, drawing, investigating, exploring, checking, or anything else you do, remember the accompanying seven steps to keep yourself away from interruptions.

1. **Pick a private space to work**

Not your bedroom, of course, in case you'd rather not feel sluggish every time you see your bed. If possible, not your living room, or if nothing else is trying to keep it clean. The disorder that surrounds us influences our concentration and reproduces a similar agitation in us. Also, in particular, the quieter the better. Nature generally works best. (if you live in town and don't have a quieter place to go, don't stop reading, hang in there for step 4).

1. **Put the telephone on mute**

Indeed, on MUTE. No vibrations. When you're working, you really want to focus on the job at hand. No story would have come out well if I had answered my mother's call or my messages in my composition. Performing various tasks is not a useful approach to work. It is a demonstrated truth. Moreover, Hector Garcia and Francesc Miralles, authors of the previously mentioned book, mention that our mind connects the vibrations of the telephone or the notification of an e-mail to the danger of a creature on the hunt. Would you like to be bothered by a ravenous lion while you work on your newest business?

1. **Switch off your telephone's WI-FI**

Late examinations have shown that a high level of twenty to thirty-year-olds go through at least 5 hours per day on their telephones. Also, I guess you imagine they didn't just visit their mate or chat on the phone for 5 hours, right? Asked by CNBC, Larry Rosen, professor of brain research at California State University, said that a large portion of us actually look at our phones like clockwork or less, whether or not we have updates. custody or warnings, because of our anxiety to pass on the open door. So the next time you need to completely focus on a mission, refrain from checking your phone by turning off the web. Minimal individual mystery, it works.

1. **Use sound-blocking earphones**

Anyway, how could it be over? Neighbors' shouts, honking, landscaping work, garbage vehicles transporting glass bottles to be reused, it happens on my road. To free myself from any disturbing influences, I put on my external noise-canceling headphones, and, unexpectedly, I am sent to another universe.

1. **Tell individuals your expectations**

It's the main propensity that you want to start having. Continuously, but consistently, let your family and friends know that you'd rather not be irritated for X hours. You can be in the quietest place imaginable, with all the warnings and the web turned off and the best music and the best headphones; assuming people are constantly traveling all over the place asking for your recommendation, your climate, or whatever, your IKIGAI stream will take off. Also, do you at least have an idea of how long it takes to get back? About 25 minutes! So please. Tell people that you have to work and that you'd rather not be upset. Sit back and relax, the people who love you understand you.

1. **Check your functioning gadget**

I have to admit, it will fill your heart with joy, a bad dream in case you don't care. I went there, I succeeded. Assuming something is wrong with your PC or any other gadget you are using, you should observe different exercises until it has calmed down or find the problem.

1. **Play a part model to begin the work**

Start your schoolwork with a decision-making propensity. I usually prefer to pay attention to Japanese piano music for 10 minutes, close my eyes, and put the spotlight on my breath. You can also light a candle, read a sonnet from your beloved writer, or recite a mantra. "I'm confident in myself. I'm as adept at anything as I can imagine" works admirably. You just need to feel free and enjoyable when you do. So what are your next plans? Train, step into your IKIGAI progression, and get the existence you need!

10
HOW TO FIND MOTIVATION

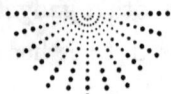

The inspiration gradually turned into a need for associations wishing to maintain a submissive and anxious workforce. Additionally, currently in the mix, the COVID-19 pandemic has undermined typical work designs and added a huge amount of general jitters just in case. It's a time of massive vulnerability, however, for many of us, it's also a potential chance to pause and reflect on our lives and the world at large. There's never been a better chance to think of your own IKIGAI.

IKIGAI can be applied as a reasonable life theory, a method for tracking down strength in troublesome times, and as a common-sense long-haul vocation organizer. It can esteem commonplace and dull exercises, while likewise assisting you with recognizing what you genuinely esteem. So how might you track down your IKIGAI?

An IKIGAI "four components" Venn chart has followed a path through office work spaces, meeting rooms, and HR introductions throughout recent years. This approach to applying IKIGAI was promoted by Albert Liebermann and Hector Garcia in their book IKIGAI. The Japanese Secret to a Long and Happy.

The chart shows IKIGAI as the combination of four daily issues: what you love, what you are good at, what the world needs, and what you can get paid for. The real goal, where each region covers, is your IKIGAI - the reason you stand up and where you should focus your efforts to seek the greatest satisfaction. Whether you are a janitor, a writer, or Jeff Bezos, if you observe your IKIGAI, you will observe the pleasure and value of what the future holds for you. Beyond your profession, IKIGAI can also be transformed into a system to get closer to life in general. Neuroscientist and creator of Tokyo, Ken Mogi, distinguishes the five pillars of IKIGAI as follows:

- Beginning little
- By tolerating yourself
- Congruity and maintainability
- The delight of easily overlooked details
- Being in the present time and place

WATCHING WHERE YOU ARE, BUT ON THE OTHER HAND, IT IS unequivocally about anticipating and savoring the exceptional moments when they arise. Where Buddhism helps you let go of the things you dream of observing opportunity and harmony, IKIGAI is more liberal, essentially training us to intentionally appreciate and enjoy things once we have them. Plus, those things can be minimal: sitting down for a nice cup of espresso, running until midday, or concentrating on the trimmed plants on the windowsill.

By following the outline of the four components, finding your IKIGAI is like observing the ideal and truly amazing line of work. Imagine joining what you love, what you excel at, what the world demands, and most importantly, what you can get paid for. Is that also possible?

TRACK DOWN YOUR CALL

This seems especially awkward if, like other people, you don't have a clue what you need for supper, let alone your last reason for living. We've all heard tales of emotional career changes in pursuit of dreams: whether it's quitting the nine-to-five to become a ski instructor or leaving a senior corporate position to retrain as a teacher. from high school. However, it doesn't have to be just intense.

Think about what sorts of exercises give you the most joy in your present place of employment:

1. Do you enjoy supervising individuals or working in confinement on specialized sites?
2. Is it true that you just deal with complicated issues or give presentations and run meetings?
3. Do you like the ability to directly supervise partners or do you like lingering over a ledger?
4. By quietly inspecting the parts of your work that you don't like and expanding on what you do, you can begin to get a feel for your IKIGAI.

SAVE THE WORLD

Yet, that covers the most troublesome viewpoint to find out: Is your specialty something the world requires? This sacrificial and liberal part of IKIGAI customarily shows itself as giving oneself to some different option from oneself. Perhaps it's not quite as troublesome as it appears from the outset, even in a lockdown period.

You don't have to leave your place of employment to retrain as a vet or begin a foundation. The main mainstay of IKIGAI helps us to 'begin little': seeking after something different can be pretty much as straightforward as offering food to your old neighbors. Or on the other hand, if conceivable, demand one free day out of every month to chip in for the wellbeing administration or give apprenticeships to hindered local area individuals.

A few minutes and signs of consideration can affect how you feel about different areas in your daily life, especially as you struggle to find inspiration. Many associations now focus on the third pillar of IKIGAI ("usability and maintainability") by assuming a "triple primary concern": to make the benefit prevail in the world and individuals in proportion to success. This way of dealing with social obligation can provide a greater sense of motivation that has an unassuming, yet strong impact. Especially on a terrible Monday morning.Track down the stream

You might feel like watching your last call is something to be grateful for, but right now you're stuck at home trying to commit to your work. Indeed, IKIGAI also supports you. Stuck at home, you probably won't be able to soak up the things that give life meaning. To fight against any later distant attitude, Ken Mogi ensures pleasure by assimilation into a movement. Work, though minor, can turn into an end in itself, not just something to persevere in order to achieve something different. Mogi uses Mihaly Csikszentmihalyi's idea of being "on the move" to edify how mingling in even the darkest races can bring a sense of reward and opportunity. (This is related to the pillars of "breaking free" and "being in present time and place"). Currently, like never before, individuals are struggling to regain their focus and inspiration. With the fulfillment that comes from being in the mainstream, even the most dreaded endeavor can become sustainable, no matter how fulfilling.

LOOK FORWARD

IKIGAI is not just about helping your vocation, it can powerfully affect inspiration and focus in the present moment, especially in times of emergency. By joining the ideal profession seeking powers of the Venn diagram, with the five main points of support, you can begin to build a new thing, capitalizing on all that conditions you in seeing yourself through difficult situations and upside down.

11
ENJOYING EVERY DAY FOLLOWING THE 5 PILLARS

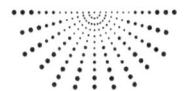

I think it's essential to keep thinking about why we get things done, to keep doing the things we do, and how we can bring more joy into our lives. The Venn chart we used is just one perspective. I found these 5 points of support much easier to think about and to achieve. The support points are:

1. Begin little, then, at that point, observe a little change that is reachable however can have an effect. Make the best of things and be pleased with it
2. Break free. Get things done, simply because you need to. Try not to act with a particular goal in mind, since that is what others expect of you. Try not to effectively get kudos for it, however, do this is because you need it.
3. Concordance and supportability, looking to live in amicability with others around you, monitoring the effect you make on them and the world. Ken Mogi (writer of "The Little IKIGAI Book") said, "Every individual's IKIGAI, when executed in amicability with others, advances inventiveness in the free trade of thoughts."

4. The delight of little things, the quest for things around you that you would regularly underestimate, however, which bring us incredible happiness when we know about it, for instance having boiling water at a tap, having a rooftop over our heads, we are encircled by things that can give us pleasure assuming we simply look.
5. Be in the present time and place, really embrace and partake in this second. Anyway, how might you grab, partake in every day more? What little change would you be able to settle on? Your joy lies in your contemplations and activities.

12
THE CONCEPT OF WABI SABI

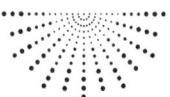

Life is capricious, acknowledge it. When nothing is sure, the sky is the limit! Your arrangements for later, in a month, or in a year may not go as planned. In any case, it is essential to make arrangements and move forward. Landon Donovan once said, "Life is flawed, obviously, however, we as a whole know how you respond to things matters." Blemish is the fundamental rule of Wabi-Sabi, the Japanese way of thinking of tolerating one's flaws and taking advantage of life.

"Wabi" is supposed to be characterized as "rural straightforwardness" or "downplayed class" with attention on toning it down would be the best mindset. "Sabi" is deciphered as "enjoying the flawed". The constant quest for flawlessness in belongings, connections, results frequently prompts pressure, tension, melancholy, and rushed judgment.

This is the place where Wabi-sabi welcomes for a break. We should be thankful for the everyday delights, and acknowledge them as they are not for what they ought to be. Wabi-sabi rewards validness. There are three basic real factors: "Nothing endures, nothing is done and nothing is awesome."

In Zen theory, there are seven stylish standards for accomplishing wabi-sabi:

- Kanso - Straightforwardness
- Fukinsei - Lopsidedness or inconsistency
- Shibumi: Magnificence in the calm
- Shizen - Unassuming effortlessness
- Yugen - Unobtrusive effortlessness
- Datsuzoku – Opportunity
- Seijaku - Serenity

The ageless insight of wabi-sabi is more applicable now than any time in recent memory to present-day life as we look for significance and satisfaction past realism. Wabi-sabi is like moderation with a cognizant decision. The idea has its underlying foundations in the customary Japanese tea function.

A typical clarification is the case of a much-adored teacup, made by the hands of a craftsman, broken or chipped from consistent use. Such follows remind the eyewitness that nothing is super durable, even fixed objects are likely to change.

A great representation of wabi-sabi in imagination is the craft of kintsugi, where broken earthenware is loaded up with gold-tidied polish as a method for showing the magnificence of its age and harm instead of concealing it.

The issue isn't covered up however featured. It is not necessarily the case that the specialist was messy (wabi-sabi is not a remotely good reason for unfortunate craftsmanship). Wabi-sabi causes to notice the breaks in a teacup as a feature of the excellence of the article. In his book "The UnknownCraftsman" SoetsuYanagi contends that defects are important for a full enthusiasm for the article and the world.

We in our human defects are dismissed by the ideal since everything is obvious all along and there is no idea of the boundless. Wabi-sabi is all over, you simply need to know what to look like and how to embrace the idea in your life.

Breaks in the old teacup are viewed as qualities rather than absconds.

"Wabi-sabi is an alternate sort of appearance, an alternate sort of attitude," clarifies Robyn Griggs Lawrence, creator of Simply Imperfect: Revisiting the Wabi-Sabi House. "It's the genuine acknowledgment of observing excellence in things as they are," he says.

Bringing Wabi-sabi into your life requires no cash, preparation, or exceptional abilities. It takes a sufficiently tranquil brain to see the value in muffled excellence, the fortitude not to fear nakedness, the eagerness to acknowledge things as they are, without decorations. It relies upon the capacity to dial back, to move the equilibrium from doing to being, to appreciation rather than flawlessness.

Mike Sturm says Wabi-sabi is related to self-tolerance and building on what you already have throughout everyday life. We must recognize ourselves in our faults.

Wabi-sabi addresses a valuable concealing spot of intelligence that values serenity, agreement, magnificence, and blemish and can fortify your strength notwithstanding realism. He tenderly allures you to unwind, dial back, make a stride back from the high-speed present-day world, and observe tomfoolery and appreciation in all that you do. Clearly, wabi-sabi allows you to act naturally. Embrace the perfection of being incomplete yourself.

13
MANDALAS

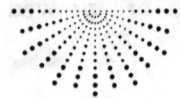

The mandala, regularly articulated as "mah-ndah-lah", is a strong otherworldly image used in stylized customs, love, consecrated craftsmanship, and contemplation. Mandalas are used by both Hindus and Buddhists to address the universe. The name comes from two separate words, "la" and "manda", which mean holder and incarnation.

If you are still wondering "what does mandala mean", I think this can help you: the term mandala is a direct interpretation of "circle" in Sanskrit. A mandala can generally be perceived by its concentric circles and other mathematical figures. Nowadays, the term mandala refers to any example or graphic with a spiral balance.

The most essential structure involves a square with four T-shaped entrances and a circle with the main problem. Either way, a mandala can illustrate other mathematical shapes, for example, triangles and polygons to frame a maze circle that has representative meaning.

MANDALA IMAGERY

Mandalas are wealthy in imagery in Hinduism and Buddhism; they bring out a significant angle in the lessons of the two religions. Whenever the priests make the mandala, they bestow the Buddha's lessons. To open the profound significance of the mandala images, a lot of further agreement is required.

On the mandala structure, there is a square sanctuary encompassed by a few concentric circles. The external circle looks like a ring of fire and represents how people are changed before they can enter the inside.

The second furthest circle is made of jewels and represents indestructibility. From that point forward, the following circle is the eight graveyards.

This circle addresses all parts of human cognizance through which people are connected with the pattern of resurrections. The internal circle is made utilizing lotus leaves, which are an image of strict resurrection.

In the middle, there is a point above which there is a picture of the primary divinity. The primary god is the focal point of the universe and has no aspects. The square sanctuary contains the embodiment of the Buddha. Inside the design, there is a castle which is for the inhabitant divinities. The sanctuary has four entryways, which are a portrayal of the accompanying belief systems:

- The four headings, to be specific north, south, east, and west.
- The four limitless considerations: compassion, sympathy, cherishing thoughtfulness, and serenity.

- One more image utilized in the mandala is a chime, which addresses female energy.

THE HOLY SIGNIFICANCE OF THE MANDALA

Mandalas are something beyond mathematical figures. The mandala isn't just wealthy in imagery yet in addition in sacrosanct importance. A consecrated figure addresses the different heavenly powers that are working known to mankind.

It addresses a sacrosanct region that fills in as a social affair point for the Hindu divine beings and as a receptor for widespread powers. Various gods involve a particular situation in the figure, making the design of the mandala extremely intricate.

These pictures are framed from the profundities of our oblivious psyche. Consequently, it can address a fantasy in analysis and the quest for solidarity and culmination of self. While intellectually entering the focal point of a mandala, the individual is emblematically offered an excursion through the universe to the substance of the real world. The mandala represents the entirety of presence, both inward and external.

During the customs, the mandala goes about as a profound aide instrument used to concentrate the adepts to prompt daze or contemplation. Mandalas are sacrosanct images that address the embodiment of the universe.

DEVELOPMENT OF THE PRIESTS MANDALA

The entire course of building a mandala is viewed as an extremely sacrosanct and reflective custom. It can take anyplace from a couple of days to a little while to finish.

At the point when priests fabricate a mandala, it assists them with partaking in the Buddha's lessons. Notwithstanding, before the priests can take part in the development of the mandalas, they should go through a significant stretch of imaginative and philosophical review. This requires around 3 years.

As is standard, four priests meet up to chip away at a solitary mandala. To work with the work, the mandala is partitioned into four equivalent quadrants, and every priest chips away at everyone. In the errand, every priest is assigned partners to fill in the tones.

A mandala is a fundamental picture in Tibetan Buddhism; it is made with a precise situation of hued sand known as dua-tson-kyil-khor in Tibetan. A mandala can likewise be built utilizing 3D bronze or stone figures, as found in China and Japan. Some are additionally made utilizing PC illustrations, yet are frequently not considered hallowed as they are made by non-Buddhists.

For the most part, a mandala is built outward from the middle where a point is. With the situation of this point in the middle, the mandala is dedicated to a specific god. Godlikeness is regularly depicted in an image above the midpoint.

For simple mathematical mandalas, lines are attracted through the middle to the four corners. This outcome is in three-sided mathematical examples. These lines are then used to construct a square royal residence with four entryways and four quadrants assigned to the four priests.

During the development of the mandala, the priests work outward in a progression of concentric circles. They work pair, moving around the mandala. Since they move outward together to guarantee balance is kept up with, they need to sit tight for one another until each segment is finished. While certain mandalas are painted after they are constructed, some are intentionally obliterated later.

Those that are painted fill in as an object of reflection. Again, those who are wiped out fill in as a sign of the temporary nature of things in customary Tibetan Buddhist education. When annihilated, the sand is filled near a watercourse like a stream to transmit positive energy.

HOW TO DRAW YOUR MANDALA?

Drawing a mandala is an important enemy of stress hobby. It assists with reaching out to your internal identity and tracking down your deepest longings through the excursion of self-disclosure. The mandala you draw could represent something you need to accomplish throughout everyday life. It can change the way we see ourselves and our motivation to live.

Other than being profoundly thoughtful, drawing a mandala liberates our inward craftsman. Different advantages of drawing your mandala incorporate passionate strength, mental lucidity, serenity, understanding, and honesty.

Before you can start drawing your mandala, you want to see how they are usually drawn. A mandala usually has a focal point in the middle. It is from here that various forms and planes arise. These depend on what's on the firm's mind and can be whatever feels good to them at the time.

Here are the materials you need to plan your mandala:

- A piece of paper or manila
- A pencil and an eraser
- A pen or indelible marker to draw on the pencil lines
- A ruler for defining boundaries

- A compass and a protractor to draw the circles. If you don't have a compass, you can utilize the covers of the round containers to make the circles.
- At long last, it would be better assuming you had a few hued pencils.
- Whenever you've assembled your materials, now is the right time to get everything rolling. On the other hand, rather than utilizing a piece of paper, you can utilize a piece of texture and finish it with weaving to make an excellent mandala plan.

Follow these means to plan your mandala:

- Observe a reasonable work surface in an undisturbed region that has negligible unsettling influence. Harmony guarantees that your imaginative energies continue to stream undisturbed.
- Settle in and ensure you are loose.
- Make a reason for your plan. Would YOU Like TO EXPRESS YOUR FEELINGS? Or then again would you like to draw the mandala for reflective purposes?
- Start by drawing an ideal square on the dark material using a pencil and a ruler. After taking the exact guesses, place a dot in the specific focus of the square.
- To help you achieve regularity, divide the image you just drew in half. This will make it much easier for you to balance by drawing on one side what you have drawn on the other side.
- Draw circles around the middle guide utilizing the compass to make them awesome and clean.
- Make different focuses at a similar separation from the middle. These new focuses ought to encase the first place

- point with the goal that they structure an ideal circle when joined. Draw more circles around these new places.
- Inside the figure, there are clear segments that you can load with any example on the picture you like. Draw any plan you can imagine.
- After you are finished with the drawing and you truly like the outcome, you can now shade your mandala as you see fit.

DRAW MANDALAS WITHOUT ANY PROBLEM

One more method for drawing mandalas is through programming called OmniGeometry. You can make however many mandalas as you need and for any reason. You can make shading pages; you can decide to draw a tattoo and any mathematical development you pick, not simply mandalas. It's so much fun to shade a mandala. After drawing it, you may need to think about shading it for an extraordinary finish.

- The various tones utilized all have various implications.
- The colors appear to be legit as well.
- Yellow represents delight, chuckling, and joy.
- Orange is for innovativeness, change, and mindfulness.
- Red addresses strength, high energy, and enthusiasm.
- Pink is for thoughtfulness, love, and womanliness.
- Purple is for otherworldliness and secret.
- Violet is for instinct and instinct.
- Blue is for internal harmony, reflection, and mending.
- Green is for actual mending, mental capacity, association, and love of nature.
- White is for immaculateness, still, small voice, and truth.
- Dark is for power, profound thought, and shadow work.

Here are some directions to assist you with making a brilliant appearance mandala:

- The first is very self-evident; you more likely than not hued pencils prepared.
- Then, you want to have a consistent brain to zero in on colors. Assuming it helps, play mitigating music to set the state of mind.
- Pick the tones you see as valuable for your motivation by following the implications recorded previously.
- Allow the shading to stream; permit him to associate with you and rouse you. The tones ought to have the option to come to you easily. Force nothing.
- Assuming you feel roused to utilize various shadings on your mandala, simply stream with it. The shadings you use imbue your mandala with significantly more prominent importance and imagery.
- As you keep on shading your mandala, simply center around how you feel as you ultimately arrive at your objective. If you are not engaged, stop. Keep shading just when the energy association returns.
- Since you have finished it, take a gander at it to feel its energy. Analyze it cautiously to check whether there are any things you might have missed while making. It is a decent sign to guarantee that you have had the right instinct if any.
- Put the last picture in someplace where you will want to see it consistently. For instance, you might have it as a wall decoration or as a screensaver for your telephone/PC. Along these lines, it will work its strong wizardry on your life consistently.
- The more profound significance of the shade of the mandala

- Colors have a unique approach to affecting how we see things and how we think. They fill different roles in Buddhist otherworldly craftsmanship.
- The shading hypothesis of Buddhism expresses that tone is an idea of edification typically addressed by unadulterated light. There are six principle tones in strict messages, five of which (all except dark) address the five representations of the Buddha. Each of the five tones happens normally.

1. White: rest, harmony, and examination
2. Yellow: sustenance and control
3. Red: accommodation
4. Blue: mending, intelligence, and life
5. Green: exorcism
6. Dark: outrage and demise

THE FIVE BUDDHA FAMILIES AND THEIR TONES

The five principle colors utilized in the mandalas compare to the 5 Buddhas and their families.

Every one of the families typifies one of the five parts of illumination and the masochist conditions of our brains of outrage, envy, obliviousness, and vanity.

1. **Vairochana**

This is the top of the Buddha family. Vairochana is a white and once in a while blue Buddha.

1. **Akshbhya**

This is the top of the Vajra family. Askshobhya is the blue and once in a while white Buddha.

1. **Ratnasambhaba**

This is the top of the Ratna or the adornments family. Ratnasambhaba is a yellow Buddha.

1. **Amitabha**

This is the top of the Padma or lotus family. Amitabha is a red Buddha.

1. **Amoghasiddhi**

This is the top of the karma or activity family. Amoghasiddhi is a green Buddha.

WHAT ARE THE PURPOSES OF A MANDALA?

They convey their exceptional kind of vibrational energy. They can, consequently, be utilized to work on one's physical, mental, profound, and passionate wellbeing. Some way or another, the mandala prompts entrancing. The mandala has a few purposes. In this part, we'll investigate two of its essential purposes:

1. **Reflection**

Mandalas are mostly utilized as an image of focus and reflection. It nearly feels like you've fallen into the shadings and begun swimming in the examples. During this second, you experience a specific delicacy.

1. **Treatment**

Clinicians and advocates utilize the mandala as an innovative apparatus during treatments. The mandala strategy permits patients to make a mandala from in a real sense anything, like sand and earth. Mandalas are an extraordinary wellspring of mending and deal with patients' various degrees of mindfulness.

The advisor can allow you to draw the mandala and shade it or shade one that has as of now been intended for you. Mandala shading has had various medical advantages for the two kids and grown-ups. Some of them include:

- In a general decrease in pressure because of lower cortisol creation (cortisol is a pressure chemical)
- Better and longer focus time
- Improvement of fine engine developments of the hands
- Lower pulse and circulatory strain
- Expanded creation and arrival of feel-great chemicals
- Numerological number cruncher

TIPS FOR A MANDALA FOR TREATMENT

Notwithstanding its example, the significance of a mandala relies chiefly upon its tone. We give you tips to test and have a good time shading a Mandala for helpful purposes.

- Having as of now picked the model, conclude which shading medium you will utilize.
- Make the shading in layers. Begin by filling a shape with a light shade, then, at that point, go over it however many times as you need until it arrives at the shade you need

- Then again, you can utilize two different hued pencils and mix them to get the ideal tone.
- Continuously apply little strain to the hued pencil to try not to break the tip.
- Assuming you tone outside the lines, utilize a white shaded pencil to cover it. These pencils will likewise assist you with filling in the valleys left behind while you were shading.
- Another incredible tip is to utilize a boring blend. This combination has no shades; it attempts to go over currently hued parts to eliminate any abundance tone or even tones. Continuously remember that there is no correct shading for treatment. The shading blends you pick are altogether dependent upon you.

REALITIES ABOUT THE MANDALA

Mandalas represent the universe. This implies that a mandala can be attracted any work of art as long as it is all around. The fundamental thought is to attempt to find yourself as you draw. Here are a few wonderful realities about mandalas to assist you with understanding them better:

1. **Appearance**

Mandalas are normal between two religions: Buddhism and Hinduism. They have likewise been seen in various ways of thinking.

1. **Significance**

Mandalas are critical in different otherworldly practices and ceremonies. Today they are utilized for remedial and mending purposes. Mandalas have been accustomed to bringing quiet and to spellbind during contemplation.

1. **Shapes**

Albeit most mandalas are portrayed with squares, they depend entirely on circles. Fundamentally, the circles are drawn from the point of convergence to alleviate pressure and any inside diseases.

1. **Domains**

A portion of the domains perceived as mandalas is Majapahit, Srivijava, Khmer, Champs, Bagan, and Ayutthaya.

1. **The five divine beings and mandalas**

The "Mandala of the Five Gods" was made in the seventeenth century. It was first found in a Tibetan artistic creation. In the middle is the RaktaYamari, additionally alluded to as the adversary of death. At the corners are the other four gods: the Yellow, the Green, the White, and the Red Yamaris.

1. **Various shapes**

The mandala arrives in a wide assortment of shapes.

1. **Self-disclosure**

Mandalas permit you to leave on an excursion of self-revelation. Significant for anybody who feels lost and needs to attempt a creative action.

1. **Portrayal**

There are no limitations on how a mandala can be addressed. You can draw it on a piece of paper, sand, texture, wall painting, or elsewhere you believe is fitting.

Additionally, a mandala is utilized to address intelligence in the universe. Examining it acutely causes you to understand a secret message inside various spirits present in the mandala.

1. **Aims**

While it is feasible to make mandalas from anything, and in some cases without a reason, there should ordinarily be a goal behind it. It would be better if you didn't make such workmanship without a reason.

1. **Available energy and tomfoolery**

Mandalas draw in its architects and watchers in a profound and self-revelation experience. Moreover, they are additionally intended for most extreme tomfoolery and diversion. This implies that you can draw a basic figure that will assist you with unwinding, which doesn't need a ton of thought.

Mandalas come in various sorts, shapes, and assortments. The two fundamental kinds of mandalas are:

- Garbha-dhatu which means "universe of the belly" in Sanskrit. In Japanese, it is known as taizo-kai and signifies "in which the development goes from one to many".
- Vajra-that, which in Sanskrit signifies "universe of jewels". In Japanese, it is known as Kongo-kai and signifies "from the numerous in one".

1. **Structural mandala**

Most structures in Tibet and Hii Malaya use mandalas to motivate plans. The design of huge stupa constructions, for example, the Jonang Monastery stupa and the Gyantse stupa are instances of the structural mandala.

Building mandalas are additionally obvious in the plan of certain mosques and houses of prayer. Essentially, their designs include a focal post around which other conelike shapes are assembled. In certain structures, the shaft can address the hub of the world.

1. **Aztec mandala**

This mandala addresses the composed type of correspondence that was recently utilized by the Aztecs. The Aztec mandala or schedule has a perplexing plan with similarly complicated importance.

The most well-known Aztec mandala is the enormous Aztec stone schedule devoted to the sun god. It estimates 12 feet in length and 3 feet thick. The Aztec mandala highlights normal social images; each addresses a divine being who decides that time.

As per their way of life, time was extremely fundamental as it directed the days and their yields. The breeze was one of the manifestations of the divine beings and is an image of knowledge. He is likewise called the god Ehacatl. The trees were made when Ehacatle fell head over heels for a human.

The light was likewise one more formation of god and represented heroes. There was likewise Tezcatlipoca, who was the divine force of dusk and, simultaneously, the lord of the north. The downpour was not just helpful to the rainforest, it likewise brought recuperating. The Storm was additionally a goddess of creation called Chalcihuilicue. He governed over storms, streams, waterways,

IKIGAI

oceans and immersion. Chalcihuilicue means "she of the jade skirt".

Here are different images on the Aztec mandala and what they address:

Blossoms addressing dance

- Rock, which addresses development, was utilized to make the shoot, weapons, and different instruments.
- Blades were normal devices in culture and represented independence in a heartfelt way.
- The reeds they gathered from the marshes addressed something educated
- The grass addressed something helpful. The Aztecs utilized grass to wind around their mats.

SKULLS ADDRESS CHANGE

- Panthers represented an incredible tracker who kills with a solitary shot.
- The deer represented traveling development and collaboration in a gathering

Bunnies implied smart and perky

- Reptiles that addressed the dynamic and dynamic perspective.
- The Ocelot addressed isolation, insider facts, and knowledge.
- Crocodiles address an ocean beast with a voracious craving that arises to make the universe. The Aztec people

group alluded to the crocodile as Cipactli. The crocodile offered them security as well.

1. **Bodhi mandala**

The expression "Bodhimandala" is utilized in Buddhism to imply a "circle of enlivening" and alludes to the region where a bodhisattva accomplishes full edification to turn into a Buddha. The Bodhi mandala idea adjusts one part of computer-generated reality.

The way that Bodhi mandalas are virtual implies that they must be underlying the internet. They are fabricated square by block by anybody, as long as they have a web association. At times, grains are utilized rather than blocks.

The virtual Bodhi mandala incorporates 8,400 squares and the people who wish can embrace the squares as long as they are accessible. The reception of a square is comparable to the acquisition of a "space".

1. **Mandala of the body**

Not at all like different mandalas, the body mandala is so unique; it is brimming with percussion and musical dynamism. Fundamentally, the body mandala is an amusement and romanticizing of the human body. The parts are envisioned to be portions of the mandala in which Buddha and different divinities dwell.

The body mandala hypothesis portrays the human body and its faculties, organs, veins, and the sensory system as an unadulterated element. Painted portrayals of the human body as a mandala are seen in the Hindu, Buddhist, Bon, and Taoist religions.

In Tantric Buddhism, the body mandala was utilized as a profound instructor to educate in major Anuttarayoga practice frameworks like Guhyasamaja, Vajrayogini, Chakrasamvara, and Hevajra Tantra.

The body mandala incorporates the mother tantra and the dad tantra. In the last option, the body mandala shows the gross body, that is to say, the appendages, arms and legs, components, and totals. These body parts are produced as parts of the structure and the different Buddha figures.

In mother tantra, the pieces of the body are produced as various channels of the inconspicuous energy framework changed into the gods and the castle. Mother tantra predominantly underlines divinities.

1. **Butterfly mandala**

The plan of the butterfly mandala is about the transformation of the bug from a caterpillar to when it turns into a butterfly. The butterfly mandala is the image of an individual's capacity to smoothly move from a past to another state.

The imagery of the butterfly is likewise focused on greatness and self-improvement.

Importance of the mandala theme

- Butterflies represent the epitome of the heavenly female that opens our energies to the lifestyle.
- Furthermore, these pieces bestow a wellspring of magnificence, elegance, and delicacy. Normal gemstones are added to gems to additional improve their recuperating and progress impacts.

Significance of the state of the mandala

- The shading choices for butterflies on mandala craftsmanship and gems are boundless. The method involved with shading a mandala is very remedial and has been displayed to assist an individual with defeating their past.

1. **Celtic mandala**

Celtic mandalas are used during reflection to define an individual's goals in Celtic groups. These address the ageless idea of the soul and show us more birth and resurrection in the physical and deeper realms. The Celtic group not only refines how we might interpret our forerunners but also enhances our ability to perceive what our activities mean to everyone around us. The Celtic twist represents deep mindfulness and understanding.

The triquetra is a three-cornered image and is utilized to address the sacred trinity. It effectively carries us nearer to God. Current devotees distinguish the Triquetra with the solidarity of psyche, body, and soul. Celtic mandalas can be found on embellishing banners, key chains, wall decorations, dishes, and domed dress plans.

1. **Christian mandala**

Mandalas are generally connected with Buddhism and different religions in Asia. The Christian mandala is a holy picture that they use to interface with the profound domain. These pictures are frequently utilized as designs and can be found on the windows of holy places and houses of God. Practically all houses of worship and basilicas have a notable glass window plan that addresses the Christian mandala.

On the other hand, in Christian engineering, a round shape is removed from the highest point of the structure to allow in light and air. The initial open to paradise represents an immediate association between the natural and otherworldly domains.

Some popular Christian mandala plans include rosaries, crowns, radiances, the fellowship has, the apsidal piece of a congregation, and some baptismal text style plans.

A typical component of this multitude of images is that they have a roundabout shape. This round shape, very much like in different mandalas, addresses the universe.

1. **Circle mandala**

The circle is the core, all things considered. Roundabout mandala plans have a wide assortment of implications; adding new circles inside a mandala gives it different importance. The motivation behind having a circle inside the mandala is for watchers to be drawn inside and feel like they are inside the mandala.

Significance of mandala painting

Roundabout mandalas are extremely valuable in assisting individuals with centering more when they think. The mandala circle represents the solidarity and completeness of heavenly nature encapsulated in man. Circles can likewise be seen as a finish or a fresh start. Roundabout mandala craftsmanship arrives in a wide assortment of shading blends and limitless examples.

This adaptability gives a cabinet such a lot of opportunity to put itself out thereby making any plan you like. Shading a roundabout mandala has incredible remedial impacts. You can paint utilizing pencils, pastels, pastels, or even charcoal.

Roundabout mandala examples should be visible joined into craftsmanship, figures, gems, artworks, and tattoos. Examples can be intricate or basic, and shadings can be intense or muffled. This all relies upon an individual's inclinations.

1. **Mandala of the roof**

Roof mandalas are typically seen on the roofs of hallowed designs like sanctuaries.

1. **Cosmological and geological mandala**

The Cosmological and Geographic mandala is the image of the four landmasses along with the Mount. Sumeru, the universe, different kinds of cosmology, hallowed domains, and unadulterated terrains, for example, Tushita, Sukhavati, Shambhala, or the Pureland Medicine Buddha. The mandala includes an inestimable outline delineating Indo-Himalayan symbolism. In the mandala is the legendary mountain, the mount. Sumeru. The mountain is addressed by a transformed pyramid with a lotus on top. The lotus represents virtue. At the foundation of the mountain are a portrayal of the sun and the moon. A three-legged bird and the moon address the sun of a hare.

1. **Mandala of heavenliness**

The mandala of heavenliness begins from Indian tantric writing and its principal intention is reflection. The mandala of heavenliness is utilized inside the Tantric Yoga hypothesis of godlikeness.

In the focal point of the god mandala is a principle figure encompassed by different figures. The term Deity is regularly utilized in Buddhism to allude to reflective and defensive divinities.

There are 3 mandalas under the heavenly nature mandala:

1. Quiet -You need to
2. Semi-quiet - Rishi
3. Irato - Rakshasa

The mandalas of the gods are accessible in the form of special necklaces that provide mileage security. These are worn on the leg or neck. Special collars can also be hung inside a vehicle or at the entrance of a house.

1. **Mandala of the components**

The mandalas of the components are earth mandalas, water mandalas, fire mandalas, wind mandalas and space mandalas. These component mandalas are simply portrayals. The earth mandala is addressed with a yellow square, water with a white circle, fire with a red crescent, and air with a blue triangle.

These five-component mandalas and their energies live inside us. They are associated with our chakras and compared to colors, feelings, thinking styles, body types, characters, and illnesses.

The mandala of the components is utilized to clarify the connection between sicknesses and their fixes. In old Indian Ayurvedic, for instance, the mandala component was the premise on which their medication was shaped.

On the mandala, the components are imagined as under the world and royal residence framework. Representation comes just after the void reflection and gets what happens when we bite the dust rather than when we are reawakened.

The brain arrives at a reasonable state where it associates with the more elevated levels of the components. The portrayal of the mandala component beneath addresses virtue of the greatest level. While survey, the components come from under the structure as clear light.

1. **Figure mandala**

As we saw before, the mandala of the figure is a piece of the mandala of eternity. The mandala accurately positions the pictures of the genuine iconographic figures around the mandala. There are two classes found under the mandala figure, which we will inspect as we come and they are:

- The upset figure mandala
- The standing mandala

1. **Mathematical mandala**

Mathematical mandalas are utilized for reflection to get a more clear perspective on life and creation overall. Mandalas are viewed as a passage between the natural domain and the heavenly domain.

While involving the mathematical mandala as contemplation, we suggest that you start with much less difficult undertakings as you progress. Otherwise, starting with complex activities will simply leave you disappointed. Mathematical mandalas are filled with layers and examples that have profound implications. Nevertheless, the circle remains the most essential shape in mathematical mandalas.

Abundance and appearance

Different shapes incorporate the crescent, triangle, and square. These structures can likewise be viewed as addressing the four components: earth, fire, water, and air.

IKIGAI

The mathematical mandala was valuable in development while building structures, particularly those considered consecrated. Notwithstanding sanctuaries, temples, and mosques, the mathematical mandala likewise motivated the Egyptian pyramids.

Mathematical mandala configuration highlights:

- A middle from which the other models transmit.
- A torus alludes to a blend of two circles that are turned around the point of convergence.
- Triangles that fill within. These join the antiquated insight of the Egyptians to the mandala.
- The blossom of life plan. This plan is framed when also estimated circles cross-over.
- Non-romantic solids. Polygons can likewise be utilized instead of Platonic solids. Their motivation is for the most part to fill the mathematical mandala.
- Lines: These break the circles to improve on the plan.

1. **Mandala of mending**

The mending mandala configuration advances profound reflection, calms pressure, and assists us with recuperating inwardly. Its plan is regularly very straightforward as it is intended to develop concentration and harmony that brings a feeling of recuperating. Assuming that the plans were extremely perplexing, they wouldn't conjure a sensation of quiet.

For quite a long time, the mandala has been utilized by specialists and advisors as a restorative instrument. They as a rule give the patient a shading activity to assist him with unwinding. The general purpose of this type of creative articulation is to support self-articulation while keeping the psyche liberated from interruptions. An illustration of the mending mandala is the yin-yang image which has demonstrated exceptionally supportive with regards to accomplishing balance in the psyche.

1. **Mandala of the heart**

The heart mandala shows some care in the middle. The heart for the most part represents fascination and love. It is likewise an image of womanliness and arousing quality, solidarity, and union. The heart mandala image can address love between family, accomplices, and companions.

The heart image has a solid association with the triangle. Thus it is additionally supposed to be connected with the component of water, which is addressed as a reversed triangle. The connection between the two methods is mystic discernment.

The tones that are utilized to additionally explain the significance of the heart mandalas are:

- Green and pink show an association with the heart chakra.
- Red shows an association with the root/power chakra.

1. **Mandala henna**

For the overall population, henna is a brief strategy for inking. Notwithstanding, henna mandalas are essential for the old Mehndi custom in Africa, India, and the Middle East.

Henna mandala craftsmanship has been around for more than 5000 years. In antiquated times, henna was applied to the arms and legs to cool the body. The formation of henna mandalas started after their shading capacities were found.

Indeed, even today, henna mandalas are a significant piece of the practice. The mehndi is as yet relevant in the present services and festivities. This training is, in its direction, an instrument of articulation. When you have henna to work with, making examples can be so motivating; there is no set-in-stone method for making a henna mandala.

1. Mandala of Jung

THIS MANDALA IS NAMED AFTER THE MOST WELL-KNOWN SPECIALIST ever. As far as he might be concerned, mandalas were accommodated limitless purposes in the treatment situation. His works in different types of craftsmanship treatment prepared for current treatment with mandalas.

Jung utilized mandalas to foster therapy in view of free articulation. Articulation in fine art is an exceptionally viable manner to separate your safeguard instrument during treatment.

These mandalas assist patients with interfacing with any interior cycles they might experience issues acquiring viewpoint on.

Today Jung is known as the "father of the advanced mandala". After him, mandalas were broadly utilized in present-day imaginative workmanship treatment.

1. Kalachakra Mandala

The Kalachakra mandala is found in the Kalachakra framework, one of the last and most complex Tantric frameworks brought from Tibet to India.

Kalachakra mandala is the sand mandala developed with shaded sand. The mandala is of a complicated nature; addresses a 5-story three-dimensional structure, which has images with exceptionally nitty gritty importance. This is what you'll view as on every one of the floors: The ground floor is the Body Mandala and has four passages looking every which way. This arrangement measures 200 by 200 spans.

The other floor is 100 understands high and elements a stage that actions 100 by 100 spans. This is the Mandala of Speech and it looks the same as the Mandala of the Body.

The center plane is the Mandala of the Mind sitting on a stage that is 50 distances over the Mandala of the Word. Size 50 by 50 spans. This arrangement is like both discourse and the body mandala.

The Mandala of Mind has two different levels: the Mandala of Exalted Wisdom and the Mandala of Great Bliss. While the previous is raised 25 arms over the Mandala of Mind and measures 25 by 25 arms, the last option is raised just somewhat over the Mandala of Exalted Wisdom.

A monster green lotus sits on the Great Bliss Mandala; this is the place where the Kalachakra Deity lives with his partner Vishvamata. Eight Shakti encompass them. From the highest point of the Great Bliss Mandala, there is a 200-foot-high rooftop.

1. **Mandala envisioned**

The envisioned mandala is just viewed as appropriate for utilizing simply by extraordinary educators and their smartest understudies. An undeniable degree of understanding is expected to utilize that. Mandalas are referenced in a few ceremonial texts.

1. **Mandala of the commencement card**

The mandalas of the commencement cards are likewise called tsakali. They allude to little canvases worked for use in Buddhist ceremonies and Bon inceptions.

A standard inception card mandala is the size of an ordinary floor tile. The mandalas of the commencement cards are utilized as the focal object of the asylum and are made when numerous inceptions are given. Such occasions are the assortments of Vajravali and Mitra Gyatsa commencements.

1. **Mandala of commencement**

These mandalas are marginally bigger than inception card mandalas. They are put on a table with other ceremonial things and contributions.

The offers are organized on the 4 edges of the table. The mandala inception is the point of convergence for the tantric commencement custom.

1. **Mandala with reversed figure**

The reversed figure mandala alludes to a mandala wherein all optional figures are standing, semi-rearranged or upstanding concerning the essential figure in the mandala.

Different figures in the creation outside the mandala circle legitimate are not viewed as a feature of the mandala. This implies that they can't be called altered.

1. **Letter Mandala**

Letter mandalas are by and large built involving letters instead of imperial divinities. They are a lot more straightforward form of the mandalas of divinities.

1. **Level mandala with divine nature**

This mandala plate is stuck to a wooden surface that is around 1 inch thick. The mandala plate with gods has a strong plan. They are primarily utilized in hallowed places or for ceremonies and commencements which are held consistently. The most widely recognized mandala plates are:

- Amitayus
- Vairochana
- Vajrayogini

The mandala plate is utilized as a contribution mandala during a custom where a contribution is made to the universe. During the custom, the dish is loaded up with rice put on the endless place of worship mandalas.

1. **Wall painting mandala**

Divider paint mandalas are painted things of beauty utilized for beautifying purposes on dividers, roofs, and other extremely durable surfaces.

Divider paint mandalas include a design look as divider compositions feature engineering components in construction by fusing them into the picture. Mandalas can be utilized to address harmony and amicability together.

1. **Painting Mandalas**

Paint mandalas or parchment mandalas are built utilizing paints and shades. They are made utilizing fine brushes to draw out the subtleties.

1. **Mandala of insurance**

Also, as the name suggests, these mandalas are used to give assurance to the people who use them.

It would be an amazing selection of gifts for the ones you love. Some authentic examples of insurance mandalas are the Tara insurance mandala and the Srid-Pa-Ho security mandala. Both of these are compelling instruments of insurance, according to Tibetan practice.

1. **Sand mandala**

A sand mandala is made with sand and incorporates numerous images and letters. Sand mandalas have generally been an impermanent type of workmanship.

Sand mandalas address temporariness throughout everyday life. Buddhist priests require days to assemble the sand mandala to the end, and when the ceremonial functions have been performed on them, the sand mandalas are destroyed.

After their deconstruction, the sand mandalas are then positioned in a waterway like a stream. In Buddhism, sand mandalas are additional images of purging and cleansing. At times, sand mandalas are developed utilizing gemstone dust.

1. **Scroll painting mandala**

Scroll painting mandalas can be rolled up and unrolled efficiently to convey them. A true illustration of the painting mandala is the "Thangka", a customary Tibetan Buddhist scroll painting. It takes a lot of perseverance to put on such a show.

1. **Sculptural mandala**

Sculptural mandalas are made with stone, metal, wood, earth, or some other material that makes a three-layered creative visual effect. Sculptural mandalas went in size from a couple of centimeters to a few meters. They were utilized in Buddhism to offer hallowed contributions. Current sculptural mandalas have added a few contemporary types of themes and address a wide scope of styles. Such figures can be utilized to supplement spaces in houses and sacrosanct spots.

1. **"Self Blessing" Mandala**

When utilized for contemplation purposes, oneself gift mandala brings out a steady gift force that keeps you in its field. Favors permit you to deal with your profound sentiments in a sweet hug.

1. **Square mandala**

The square design in the center addresses a protected spot with an equilibrium in contrary energies. The square mandala represents the middle, which is a gathering place. It contains the embodiment of the Buddha and has a castle which is the home of the gods present. The square has four entryways that represent different thoughts, similarly as we found in the starting piece of this piece.

The square mandala represents the middle which is a gathering place. It contains the quintessence of the Buddha and has a castle that houses the deities present. The plaza has four entrances that represent an assortment of pansies similar to those we found in the initial piece of this room.

1. **Mandala image**

Image Mandalas are exceptionally improved on adaptations were rather than drawing the genuine divinities, hand credits are utilized. While drawing the image mandalas, just the images addressing the divinities are utilized; the figures beneath are filled in utilizing little painted circles. Now and then, there isn't anything by any means to show the presence of the accompanying figures.

1. **Cross mandala of strings**

The interweaved mandala is likewise called Namka. It comprises dainty bits of wood on an edge wrapped with strings of different shadings. The bits of wood meet up to frame different shapes and examples which are shown upward. Typical string cross mandalas are level, while some are truly made in three-dimensional to celebrate customs.

1. **Mandala in standing figure**

The standing mandala has a few auxiliary figures remaining regarding the focal figure of the synthesis as opposed to the transformed figure mandala. The focal figure of the piece is viewed as the single observer of the synthesis.

1. **Yantra Mandala**

The Yantra Mandala highlights special 2-D or three-dimensional mathematical plans; The imagery of these mandalas has a rich custom. Mandalas are effectively utilized for thoughtful purposes in Vajrayana Buddhism. Before an individual can arrive at a condition of edification, he should make the way to divine powers. Doing this permits an individual to turn out to be entire and, thusly, to work inside the energies of the universe.

1. Lotus mandala

THE LOTUS MANDALA IS A THREE-DIMENSIONAL FIGURE MADE OF metal. It includes a sprouting lotus and a stem that goes about as a help. This thing of beauty expects that you center around it to accomplish harmony. The lotus is a bloom that is accepted to have many layers, which represents the way of life of East Asia.

Lotuses are essential for various mandalas since they have a significant degree of intricacy, which fits impeccably with the complex mathematical plan of mandalas. Some famous mandala plans that include a lotus are:

- Sri Yantra
- GaneshaYantra
- Harpoon Yantra
- Garbhadhatu Mandala
- Nava Padma Mandala

1. Blossom mandala

There are countless various sorts of flower mandalas. Some have a solitary bloom whose petals emanate outward. Different plans have many blossoms of various sizes and tones.

The botanical mandala includes a progression of covering circles that structure blossoms all through the mandala. The mandala is otherwise called hallowed calculation and is accepted to bring otherworldly illumination.

Here is a rundown of a few normal botanical mandalas and their imagery:

White Rose

The white rose is regularly connected with otherworldly arousing.

Pink dahlia

This bloom is an image of self-esteem.

White Lily

This botanical mandala addresses our decisions and choices.

Blue morning magnificence

This bloom addresses effortlessness as it were that brings harmony.

Red Begonia

This bloom is an image of equilibrium

1. **Mandala of the sun**

Now and again, the sun mandala is additionally used to address innovativeness and energy. Sun mandalas portray light beams emanating from the middle to the external ring of the mandala. These spokes come in various sizes and are wavy or straight. A portion of the normal sun mandalas are:

- Yantra brilliant sun
- VitalitySunYantra
- Sun Creative Energy
- Love SunYantra

Sun mandalas are utilized for profound purposes, yet in addition as improving pieces.

14
A ONE MINUTE MEDITATION YOU CAN DO ANYWHERE

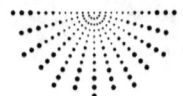

It could shock you to observe that in 60 seconds you can reset your mentality. Doing a brief contemplation can be inconceivably successful as it offers us an ideal chance to have some time off, move away from what we are doing, inhale profoundly and re-energize. Moreover, committing one moment daily is open to even the most active individual.

THE MOST EFFECTIVE WAY TO DO A BRIEF REFLECTION

This is how you can experience the benefits of contemplation in just 60 seconds. Observe a pleasant sitting position, whether you are at home, at work, outdoors, or at any other event, sitting in the vehicle on the left. Then, at that moment, close your eyes and focus on your breathing. Breath control in a brief reflection is very valuable because of the quick mental association, which makes for a more stable perspective. Presently center quietly around counting your breaths or looking at your body. Permitting yourself to inundate yourself profoundly in your psyche and body briefly can assist with your navigation, concentration, correspondence, and energy levels.

Attempt this brief contemplation to dispose of pressure. Eating with faculties: Engage each of your faculties before partaking in a feast. Try not to be listless, sixty seconds into the economy of the day doesn't mean a major exercise in futility. Anyway, it is certain that with this training, you will want to work on the nature of your days. After attempting a few one-minute thoughts, do it effectively and consistently. It can help you start unlocking a lot more benefits.

15
THE LONG ROAD OF IKIGAI

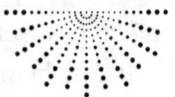

The Japanese specialty of kintsugi includes the maintenance of broken ceramics with gold leaf to deliver something more valuable and lovely than the first. Flaws are important for the person and excellence of the new work of art.

The way we live, actually and professionally, can also separate. Another Japanese practice, IKIGAI, can help us recover and regain sanity. Like the kintsugi, it offers a seriously satisfying, comprehensive, and valuable package.

Tracking down an immediate interpretation for the Japanese word IKIGAI and, maybe more significantly, the ethos behind it isn't clear. IKIGAI can be perceived as a "composite develop, which incorporates importance, inspirations, and values throughout everyday life," say the scientists.

Running and partaking in a movement and our life object are all IKIGAI, originating from profound attention to the accompanying:

- Energy: what you love
- Work: what are you great at
- Mission: what the world necessities
- Calling: What you can get compensated for

As indicated by Yukari Mitsuhashi, IKIGAI isn't just about our overall objectives and significance throughout everyday life, except is found in individual minutes and interest in each part of our lifestyle.

HOW MIGHT IKIGAI HELP US?

The customary and getting through the Japanese lifestyle addressed by IKIGAI might bring a great deal to the table for our cutting-edge lifestyle. Thus, there has recently been an expansion of research focusing on IKIGAI as a method of seeing as "motivation to live", but also, all the more so overall, on certain outcomes related to well-being. to be.

Notwithstanding, despite the fact that it is hard to nail down, its advantages are turning out to be progressively obvious when joined with positive brain science and preventive medication. As a matter of fact, research has observed that IKIGAI is a valuable indicator of both physical and mental prosperity.

For sure, the constructive outcomes of IKIGAI are seen in numerous parts of life, including:

- Actual wellbeing in the older
- Mental prosperity of carers
- Diminished occurrence of stroke and cardiovascular illness
- Emotional wellness

All things considered, while IKIGAI is a complex and intricate development, our relationship with it probably won't be as simple as a presence or absence.

ESTIMATING THE IKIGAI SURVEY

IKIGAI is private and explicit to every one of us, it addresses where our central goal, employment, and expert life meet.

SO HOW COULD IT BE ESTIMATED?

Despite its importance and the total assortment of exploration in Japan, it seems, by all accounts, that there aren't many immediate and solid western proportions of IKIGAI.

IKIGAI-9 POLL

The IKIGAI-9 poll and psychometric apparatus are both advantageous and solid, as they measure IKIGAI across numerous aspects:

- Hopeful and positive feelings towards life.
- Dynamic and inspirational perspectives towards one's future.
- Acknowledgment of the significance of one's presence.

IKIGAI comprises nine explanations to score against and is accordingly somewhat easy to finish.

- I frequently feel cheerful.
- I might want to gain some new useful knowledge or begin something.
- I feel like I am adding to somebody or society.
- I have space for myself.

- I'm keen on numerous things.
- I think my reality is fundamental for a person or thing.
- My life is intellectually rich and satisfied.
- I might want to create.
- I think I'm affecting someone.

By estimating IKIGAI, it is feasible to recognize, investigate and comprehend the positive effects of IKIGAI-put together mediations with respect to psychological wellness.

BY WHAT OTHER MEANS COULD WE QUANTIFY THE IKIGAI

Estimating related ideas like a stream: our total assimilation into a movement and our general fulfillment in life can likewise offer more data on the best way to carry on with a day-to-day existence all the more completely and with reason.

- IKIGAI specialists Héctor García and Francesc Miralles (2018) write that although there is no reliable life option in daily life according to IKIGAI, flow is a key solution that allows us " appreciate accomplishing something such a lot of that we neglect any concerns we may have while we make it happen. " The flow and vibrations of an ideal encounter are more likely when "the necessities of the errand and the abilities of the entertainer are adjusted".
- Challenge-ability balance
- Activity mindfulness combination
- Clear objectives
- Interesting input
- Focus on the errand
- Feeling of control
- Loss of mindfulness

- Change of time

Every one of the accompanying assertions is related to a particular action and delegated Never, Rarely, Sometimes, Frequently, or Always.

- While taking an interest in [business name], I know what I need to do.
- My consideration is centered totally around the thing I am doing.
- It doesn't matter to me what others could imagine me.
- Things appear to happen consequently.
- I observe the experience as very fulfilling.

Broadly approved, DFS-2 offers a pragmatic way to deal with estimating dispositional stream (the inclination towards such encounters) and the capacity to enter ideal mental states, and is accordingly predictable with IKIGAI. Accomplishing the mental conditions of the stream makes everyday exercises remarkable and assists you with benefiting from your IKIGAI.

FULFILLMENT WITH THE STEPPING STOOL OF LIFE

Although not an immediate proportion of IKIGAI, life fulfillment is intertwined and comparably affects prosperity. The Life Satisfaction Scale, a tiered model of a mental thriving, was used in the Japanese IKIGAI exam to assess worldly life thriving and positive mental work.

People study each of the five accompanying statements and give a fair assessment of their arrangement using a scale between 1 and 7 (where 1 strongly differs and 7 strongly conflicts).

- In numerous ways, my life is near my ideal.
- The states of my life are incredible.
- I'm happy with my life.
- Up until this point, I've gotten the significant things I need throughout everyday life.
- Assuming I could remember my life, I would change barely anything.

The collected scores demonstrate the degree of fulfillment with life, between the accompanying two limits:

1. Individuals who love their life.
2. Things are noticeably flawed however they can be moved along.

INDIVIDUALS WHO ARE VERY DISAPPOINTED WITH THEIR LIFE

Either an aftereffect of a new bombshell (demise of a friend or family member or joblessness) or long haul disappointment with numerous parts of their life. The reactions and in general scores give important data and direction to future activity and learning experiences. The assistance of specialists, instructors, and analysts can be incredibly useful for people who are to some degree or very disappointed with their life.

4 TESTS YOU CAN UTILIZE

Appreciate what you are doing in light of the fact that IKIGAI expects you to know yourself; it is fundamental to understand your qualities, what is important to you, and your needs. They are profoundly deprived of what their identity is. Questions you want to ask yourself:

1. Do what you like?

What did you jump at the chance to do as a kid or in your initial a very long time as a grown-up?

What do you do now in the leisure time that fulfills you?

1. Do what you're great at?

Do you know your assets and abilities? Which ones would they say they are?

What truly do individuals request that you assist them with?

1. Accomplish something the world requirements

What and who motivates you?

What makes you irritated or baffled?

1. Accomplish something you can get compensated for

What administration or item would you be able to sell (what could people pay you for)?

What work would you be able to do?

First, compose the responses on a piece of paper, then, at that point, momentarily sum up and move them to a clear IKIGAI outline: Invest energy assessing the finished outline and consider which movement squeezes into the middle, meeting every one of the four circle standards.

TRACK DOWN YOUR MOTIVATION

Frequently automatically, we give our very best in our waking hours, halting just to crash before the TV or get into bed. IKIGAI urges us to zero in on the universally useful of our life and the "delight individual views as in living every day" (Mitsuhashi, 2018).

Answer these questions:

- When I was a kid, I loved having the opportunity to...
- In case money doesn't make a difference, I'll be...
- If I thought I couldn't be short, I would...
- I totally forget about time when I'm ...
- I'm extremely content with who I am when ...
- I'm great at ...
- On the off chance that I didn't mind others' thought process of me, I would ...
- In my leisure time, I like to...
- On the off chance that I was just a half year old, I'd invest my energy ...
- If I somehow managed to pass on tomorrow, I would lament not having done as such ...
- The accompanying individuals move me on the grounds that ...

Audit finished sentences, adding new ones when you ponder them. See the examples that structure and perceive the activities that go with past exercises and likely arrangements. Then, at that point, finally, complete another sentence:

The reason for my life is to ...

Utilize the full sentence to help you consider and direct your future choices. If you shape your life as indicated by the reason you have found, you will show up at IKIGAI. There are online tests accessible that can help you find and foster your IKIGAI.

While a portion of the assets is free, installment or enrollment might be expected to get extra counsel and instruction. Making stream encounters is a method for making and participating in stream encounters that are intrinsically remunerating with the possibility to accomplish an ideal mental state.

Stream investigation encounters can be utilized with clients to more readily get the nature and qualities of the stream. Addressing needs in various everyday issues assists you with considering your requirements and the degree to which they are being met.

As Tim Tamashiro (2019) composes, "IKIGAI is inside the scope of us all and can fill in as a guide to find and make reason." Answering the questions in this section will help you find sanity and happiness in everyday existence, but there is no simple change that makes everything good.

At last and in particular, we should secure adequate self-information to have the option to finish the accompanying two sentences:

"I feel IKIGAI when ..."

"I feel IKIGAI towards ..."

Whenever we can give an unmistakable and complete (and individual) proclamation for everyone, we will be prepared to assemble IKIGAI at each phase of our reality. In this way, toward the finish of life, we can think back with general fulfillment and a reasonable feeling of living as per our requirements and needs. Maybe we will have lived all the more genuine and less directed by the upsides of others.

While there are no convenient solutions, with regards to IKIGAI, little changes can prompt significant changes, over the long run, in our (or our clients') lives. As Tim Tamashiro says, truth be told, "Whenever you put your finger on what your IKIGAI is, it resembles getting a superpower [...] a GPS for your life."

"IKIGAI is the move we make in the quest for bliss." Once known, we can make more certain short-and long haul choices, actually and expertly, by making an existence with more reason (Mitsuhashi, 2018).

Lastly, as indicated by Mitsuhashi, while having and feeling IKIGAI is interesting to you and is a likely wellspring of bliss, it is just accessible through activity and not just by sitting tight for it to occur.

16
TIPS FOR ACHIEVING IKIGAI

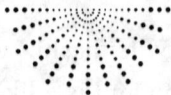

As indicated by the Japanese practice, each individual has an IKIGAI, a justification for living. At the point when you observe your IKIGAI, where energy, calling, and reason cross, you track down significance in regular daily existence. Track down the bliss of continuously being occupied.

We discovered a few critical ideas to assist with busying individuals all over the place, including occupied guardians, foster their feeling of IKIGAI, and track down happiness in their day to day routines:

1. **Ensure you like what you do**

Many individuals fantasy about getting a new line of work they love when the key to joy lies in flipping around this thought: observing something pleasant in all that you do. It is an issue of viewpoint.

1. **Reflect on the go**

Assuming that your timetable expects you to be continually in a hurry, exploit your movements and use them to do reflective activities. Take a stab at becoming mindful of your body as it moves as you stroll (without taking a gander at the telephone), examining your environmental factors through Mindfulness as you move and focusing

1. **Account for your IKIGAI**

Nobody is occupied to the point that they can't require 30 minutes to peruse a book, go for a stroll in the recreation area to revive their contemplations or do some action that re-energizes the batteries of their spirit.

1. **Separate the critical things from the significant things**

Critical things are vital to others, however, they are not generally vital to us and can lead us to neglect to focus on our needs and focus just on the needs of others.

1. **Try not to accept commitments during your available energy**

As well as working a greater number of hours than they would like, many individuals today commit to responsibilities during their spare energy that winds up causing their life to appear to be turbulent like a Marx Brothers film. Deal with those responsibilities that are essential and that cause you to feel cheerful and set liberated from the rest. As Steve Jobs said, "Your time is restricted, so don't squander it living another person's life."

1. **Follow a kind of computerized diet**

Besides, hyperconnection opens us to a steady torrential slide of data, a lot of it negative. Being disconnected for a couple of hours daily is exceptionally gainful for a sound mental nature, particularly before nodding off.

1. **Follow your interests**

Toward the finish of their life, nobody feels pleased with having worked vast hours. Rather we recall with a grin every one of the insane things, of all shapes and sizes, that we have allowed ourselves to do. Put experience into your life by voyaging, finding, or learning new things.

If you foster your secret abilities and offer them to others, you will live in IKIGAI.

17
HOW TO FIND YOUR IDEAL JOB WITH THE IKIGAI METHOD

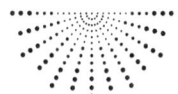

*A*t any point do I stare off into space while sitting before a PC screen attempting to work? You keep thinking about whether you might have had an incredible vocation in money or design. Or on the other hand, perhaps you might have been a craftsman. On the off chance that you hadn't quite contented when you were nine, you may be a swimming hero now. Consider the possibility that you haven't tracked down the correct way yet. IKIGAI is a Japanese idea that can assist you with assessing the situation and tracking down your motivation. Of all the self-awareness strategies that are well known right now, this one is entirely available. So it merits a look.

A LITTLE FOUNDATION DATA

IKIGAI's attitude, which traces back to the fourteenth century, clarifies the long future individuals of Okinawa Island, which is otherwise called "the island of immortals". As far as they might be concerned, having the motivation to get up in the first part of the day is the way into a healthy lifestyle, when matched with a sound eating routine and normal active work. IKIGAI assists you with tracking down the crossing point between what motivates you, what drives you, and your goals.

APPLYING IT TO THE EXPERT REGION

With regards to your expert life, observing your IKIGAI implies getting a new line of work that satisfies you, and that you view as significant. Since the last option is viewed as the Holy Grail, you might have come to see this thought as just an unrealistic fantasy. Here is the uplifting news: We all have an IKIGAI and it's generally simple to find.

You can relax, it won't mean getting everything together so you can appear for a tryout for The Voice. In her book, Find child IKIGAI (Find Your IKIGAI), writer Christie Vanbremeersch clarifies that it is important to "move from a sensation of trickiness and impoverishment to blissful thriftiness". Truth be told, the people who are enthusiastic about their work are generally ready to make monetary penances. You observe your IKIGAI when you focus on your self-awareness rather than material things. Whenever you comprehend your motivation, you can accomplish balance in your own and proficient life while tolerating the possibility that acquiring less can assist you with carrying on with a superior life. Before evolving, ask yourself these questions vocation Change:

- Is It the Right Time?
- So how would you get your IKIGAI?

Alright, we should incorporate the hypothesis. The Japanese strategy includes posing yourself four significant inquiries so you can decide your IKIGAI and your motivation. Your responses will hypothetically cover in the center. To respond to these inquiries in a non-shallow and useful manner will require a great deal of time. Regardless of whether it was a long time everything looks great, take constantly what you need.

1. What do you get a kick out of the chance to do?

Make a rundown of all that brings you happiness consistently. Try not to restrict this rundown. Compose everything down. You could likewise ponder who you are desirous of and why. IKIGAI experts say that observing the correct way at times implies going through torment, dissatisfaction, outrage, or other troublesome sentiments, which might be horrendous right away, however is useful while starting change.

1. What are you great at?

You may not see it, yet individuals likely consistently praise you. Perhaps they like your cooking, your physicality, your innovativeness, or your melodic ability. Perhaps you are known for your relationship abilities: showing restraint, kind, or liberal. Attempt to distinguish regions that require these particular abilities.

1. What do you do that assists you with making money?

It is continuously intriguing to assess your expert abilities. What is a portion of the things you do consistently? For what reason do you get compensated to make them? What different abilities or capacities do you have that you could get compensated to utilize?

1. What is it that the world needs?

Could it be said that you are on top of your environmental elements? Are there any causes or issues that worry you or concern you? Things you might want to change or causes you might want to engage with assistance?

The circumstance wherein you will prosper is at the intersection of the responses to these four inquiries, where your interests are entwined with your motivation, your calling, and your employment. Compose your responses in a circle that addresses every one of these inquiries, and your IKIGAI will be at the junction. From these components, it is valuable for you to make, design, and adjust to a truly amazing job and the existence that goes with it!

18
REDISCOVERING THE PASSION FOR WORK

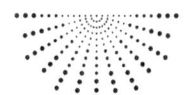

You have lost your enthusiasm for work, IKIGAI could assist you with rediscovering it. What is the explanation you get up toward the beginning of the day? What is your motivation throughout everyday life? Where do your qualities, interests, convictions, and gifts cover? "IKIGAI alludes to the things that acquire happiness in your life," says Ken Mogi, a Japanese neuroscientist, and writer of The Little Book of IKIGAI.

"IKIGAI is an apparition, from little delights to enormous life objectives. IKIGAI can be a private satisfaction as well as something socially significant. All the time, IKIGAI is the explanation you get up in the first part of the day. " A portion of the world's longest-lived residents dwell in Japan, and IKIGAI is remembered to add to life span, in Japan, however all over the planet (regardless of whether they have a word). Once more, there are four standards of IKIGAI:

1. What you love (enthusiasm and mission).
2. What are the world requirements (mission and livelihood)?

3. What are you good at (energy and calling).
4. What you can get compensated for (calling and employment).

If you are considering a Venn outline with these four standards, where the four circles intersect is your IKIGAI." IKIGAI gives your life inspiration while giving you the oomph to push ahead," says Mogi.

FOR WHAT REASON DOES IKIGAI RESOUND WITH SO MANY?

Mogi accepts IKIGAI is a cure to the pressure and mental tensions of living in a bustling world. "Under the economy of globalization, individuals feel increasingly more forced to improve their lives," he says. "However, achievement doesn't come to everybody".

The standards behind IKIGAI perceive that private delights in your day-to-day existence may not have social importance or convert into your expert life. "At the point when you have IKIGAI, you are probably going to have better execution, acknowledging stream and mindfulness," says Mogi. "What's more, thus, you might be socially effective, yet that is a reward. Regardless of whether you [at work], you actually have IKIGAI. "

IKIGAI isn't about acknowledgment or recognition, but instead, it is tied in with beginning little and following the things that give you joy. As indicated by Mogi, there are five mainstays of business that permit IKIGAI to flourish:

1. Beginning little (zeroing in on the subtleties).
2. Break free (acknowledge your assets and defects).
3. Tracking down concordance and maintainability (interfacing with others).

4. Perceive the delight of little things (appreciate taste, contact, smell, sight, and hearing).
5. Being in the present time and place.

Mogi says these five support points support the quintessence of IKIGAI and can be applied to any of the four standards. "In the event that you apply the five mainstays of the business to the crossing point, you will get more IKIGAI," says Mogi.

APPLY IKIGAI TO YOUR PROFESSION

Youth work is playing and Mogi trusts that assuming somebody has lost their enthusiasm for work, they should begin by pondering adolescence or on when life appeared to be easier. "IKIGAI resembles resuscitating the internal identity," he says. "What were the things that brought you happiness? What did you appreciate doing, with next to no thought of social significance or commitment to your possible achievement? "

Youngsters are normally attracted to the exercises and individuals they appreciate with little respect to how they are seen or the finished result. "Getting back to the bits of knowledge of the internal identity would give the important recovery and restore your enthusiasm for living completely," says Mogi.

You can characterize and seek after your IKIGAI, without requiring the endorsement or authority of others. In any case, says Mogi, talking about your IKIGAI with loved ones can assist with understanding IKIGAI's rich variety among individuals. "Beginning little typically gets the job done," he says. "Assuming you follow your IKIGAI bits of knowledge sincerely, little activities frequently lead to huge things."

19
EXERCISES

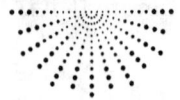

To give up

Stand up, sit, or rest in a comfortable position by placing your hands gently on your stomach. Breathe in leisurely and profoundly through the nose and afterward out through the mouth multiple times. Feel your midsection tenderly lift as you breathe in and afterward fall once more. Each time you breathe out, free yourself from the pressure of the day by intellectually telling yourself: "I let it go." Envision each pressure, each unsettled inclination, each weight on your shoulders taking off with your breath. Ok! To complete the activity, smile.

Gold sign

The accompanying inquiries can give you a major lift as you continued looking for your IKIGAI. They resemble a brilliant sign demonstrating the correct bearing. When you are prepared, you can begin.

Find an agreeable position once more, do the breathing activity, or simply unwind, then, at that point, center your psyche around the accompanying inquiries. What were your beloved activities as a child and what did you like about them? Compose something like two reactions.

1. My beloved activities as a child were....
2. What I preferred about these things.

You are amidst an innovative approach. Memories for you have probably already called for a lot of pictures. Use that second to skip straight to the next survey.

WHAT WERE YOUR BELOVED ACTIVITIES AS A TEEN?

You can put a wide range of things down here. Assuming you are delighted in exploring different avenues regarding a science set, appreciate skating or going the entire evening time playing with the PC. What side interests were truly fun, how did you manage your companions? Go ahead and compose things that could appear to be extremely ordinary, such as paying attention to music, moving, gazing at the outer layer of a lake for a long time, or perceiving shapes in the mists overhead - as a component of your rundown.

My cherished activities as a youngster were

Clarify again why you delighted in doing these things.

What I loved about these things

Also, what were your cherished activities as a youthful grown-up? The second you began assuming control over life, perhaps you ventured out from home, found the world increasingly more all alone? Here as well, list somewhere around three things.

My cherished activities as a youthful grown-up were

What I enjoyed about these things

Incredible. After this surge of memories and images, we must now move on to the next step. You are allowed to use your insight abilities now. Review your reactions to what you liked about your favorite exercises, each in turn. What topics get dwelled on, what's still vital to you that feels predictable and straightforward?

Introduce these things by underlining catchphrases or messages in an alternate tone. Whenever you are done, you can go through the last advance. Take a look at the key messages you presented and think about what data you can glean from them. Try to put these ends in extremely short words and jot them down in the list of topics below.

Let me reveal this interaction to you using a template from my recaps. As a youngster, one of my cherished activities was climbing trees. My recap of what I enjoyed looks like this: I felt free and had a solid feeling of association with the tree and the woodland all in all; I partook in the sensation of being "above things" taking a gander at the world from a higher place and pursuing my considerations; I was additionally glad to conquer my apprehensions and feel my solidarity as I rose.

Then, at that point, I contemplated what these key messages say about me and noticed the accompanying in my rundown. The sensation of opportunity and experience, association with nature, searching for new viewpoints, thinking/pondering something, beating limits, self-effectiveness, self-confirmation, and active work.

Indeed, I figured out how to get a wide range of angles out of one most loved action. Yet, they have a major impact on my life today. I'm generally astounded at how precise the bits of knowledge we can help about ourselves are through this basic activity. Maybe we stir a specific world to us while making these rundowns, a world brimming with tones, potential outcomes, and guarantees, yet additionally a position of extraordinary clearness. A world that we regularly can't completely access in our day-to-day routines, because the street is obstructed by innumerable solicitations and commitments, stress and pressure, and the sensation of continuously being occupied.

What's more, presently it's your turn once more. Invest in some opportunity for this progression, however, kindly don't pressure if you can't get a ton of viewpoints out of one of your beloved exercises. In some cases, we can perceive a few subjects and in some cases, there is just one to see. All that is significant is that you investigate why you delighted in following through with something. Look through the featured top messages and enter your bits of knowledge into the rundown beneath.

RUNDOWN OF SUBJECTS

Assuming you've arranged all of the preparation units records today, you've gained great headway. Presently you can have some time off and put the book down. Assuming you have a great deal of energy, go ahead and proceed. Be that as it may, generally ensure you do the activities when you feel intellectually endlessly ready.

Somebody truly prefers to compose, loves to write their contemplations down and make entire awesome universes, and perhaps has a message they might want to impart to other people. This implies that her main goal is to engage and move others with her accounts and to change the world in the little.

Assuming he tracks down a distributor to distribute his books, that mission turns into a calling. Furthermore, assuming his books offer an adequate number of duplicates to earn enough to pay the rent composing, that would be preferable.

It is additionally conceivable that this individual would rather not track down a distributor; he simply composes for no particular reason. He could independently publish his accounts or offer them on a blog, allowing the world to get something out of them in an alternate manner.

He earns enough to pay the rent by different means, however, throughout the long term, his blog gets an ever-increasing number of snaps and is at last found by a distributer, permitting him to invest more energy composing. A comparable situation could happen with recordings that somebody transfers to an Internet stage for no reason in particular.

The videomaker likes to get it done, he allows others to partake in his motion pictures, and the event that all works out in a good way and his recordings get a ton of snaps he could even bring in cash out of it.

As I clarified, the singular angles in the various regions can immensely affect our IKIGAI. Yet, whenever you've observed a convincing junction in the graph, it shouldn't be excessively difficult for you to respond to the inquiries: What do I get up for toward the beginning of the day? What makes my daily routine fulfilling and worth experiencing? What gives it meaning?

20
THE IKIGAI DIET

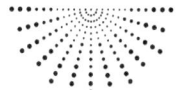

*I*KIGAI diet eating routine of Japanese centenarians, is an eating regimen wealthy in fiber, to a great extent plant-based, wealthy in what the future held superfoods. Whenever we consider Japanese centenarians, Okinawans ring a bell. Notwithstanding, Okinawa doesn't have the biggest number of centenarians per capita. This honor goes to Shiga Prefecture. Japan has almost 70,000 centenarians, with around 15% living in significant urban communities, like Tokyo and Osaka, while the rest live in Japan's numerous provincial regions.

These centenarians ordinarily eat a conventional eating routine of rice, miso soup, pickles, bubbled or prepared vegetables, fish, and soy food varieties like tofu or natto. Japanese centenarians eat neighborhood, meaning they source food like vegetables from their nearby regions or much of the time from their nurseries.

Japanese centenarians don't:

- They eat quick or low-quality food
- They eat handled food sources

- Eat or drink sugar
- They eat excessively

JAPANESE SUPERFOODS

Japan has an overflow of supplement thick food. In the West a significant number of them are hailed as superfoods, however, for the Japanese, these are simply normal fixings or side dishes of their everyday dinners.

- Beans
- Miso
- Tofu
- Natto
- Adzuki
- Kuromame
- Kinako
- Vegetables
- Daikon
- Yam
- Goya
- Kobocha
- Negi
- Renko
- Gobo
- Kelp
- Noriu
- Wakame
- Kombu
- Hijiki
- Mekabu
- Mushrooms - Mushrooms
- Shitake

- Enokitake
- Mitake
- Matsutake
- Shimeji
- Lord shellfish
- Nameko
- Rice

- Genmai
- Zakokkumai
- Natural product
- Umeboshi
- Yuzu
- Wasabi
- Shiso
- Goma
- You
- Matcha
- Hojicha

WAYASAHII WIZARD: MY GRANDCHILDREN ARE CARING

The Japanese expression entertainer wayasashii means "grandkids are benevolent", performer implies grandkids, yasashii implies kind, and wa is the subject pointer. In any case, the expression is additionally utilized as a typical Japanese re-arranged word with every syllable MA-GO-HA-YA-SA-SHI-I addressing a significant Japanese food or food.

. . .

Mama - Mame (Beans)

A vital piece of the Japanese eating regimen, beans are high in protein, nutrients, and fiber. Natto, aged soybeans, is one of the most outstanding Japanese superfoods.

GO - Goma (sesame seeds)

Sesame seeds are plentiful in calcium, fiber, protein, and minerals. Thusly, they are viewed as one of Japan's enemies of maturing food sources. They are best utilized or served on the ground.

WA - Wakame (Algae)

Wakame is likely the most consumed kelp in Japan. Wakame contains minerals, proteins, nutrients, and fiber. Wakame gives your hair and nails an energetic sparkle!

YA - Yasai (vegetables)

Japan has numerous one-of-a-kind vegetables: daikon, goya, renkon, and gobo to give some examples. The Japanese know the significance of eating a wide assortment of vegetables.

SA - Sakana (fish)

The Japanese eat a ton of fish - sashimi, sushi, barbecued fish, and so forth Fish is ready in various ways in Japan to remove the supplements and flavors. Fish gives a significant wellspring of amino acids and iron.

SHI - Shiitake (Mushrooms)

Shiitake mushrooms are plentiful in protein, fiber, vitamin D, and vitamin B. As a concentrate, shiitake mushrooms are utilized to fortify the invulnerable framework and lower blood cholesterol levels.

I - Imo (potato)

A significant wellspring of sugars, potatoes contain nutrients and minerals. Japanese yams are profoundly nutritious and are a brilliant wellspring of fiber, nutrients, and minerals. They likewise advance stomach wellbeing.

IT'S NOT JUST ABOUT FOOD

The IKIGAI diet isn't just about the food that the Japanese eat, yet additionally about the traditions they practice when they eat. Japanese individuals profoundly regard food and offer thanks when every feast. They are likewise exceptionally cautious about squander. It would be an interesting sight to see an uneaten grain of rice.

21
THE SECRETS OF THE OKINAWANS

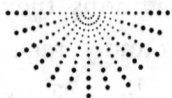

The Yoga and healing specialists serenade "om" as a long and happy life mantra. Others sing supercalifragilistic-expialidocious. In any case, occupants of the Japanese island of Okinawa have different words that are demonstrated ideas for a cheerful life span: IKIGAI, moai, and harahachibu.

These are influential ideas that can assist you with having a more significant and enduring retirement. Who are the Okinawans and what do they are their familiar life span? Okinawa is an island south of the central area of Japan, where the East China Sea meets the Pacific Ocean. It is a wonderful tropical spot with probably the longest living people on the planet. All things considered, men live to 84 and ladies to 90. There is likewise an exceptionally high grouping of centenarians. Maybe most shockingly, even Okinawan seniors are viewed as solid and have the enthusiastic, physical, and mental ability to live and work freely.

SO WHAT'S THEIR MYSTERY?

Analysts say Okinawan insider facts include: IKIGAI, moai, and harahachi bu. What if we found out what these fascinating words mean. Moreover, as we have said, IKIGAI is "motivation to live". In addition, they are more motivated and versatile, which protects them from stress and burnout. It's trying for you.

Your IKIGAI should be something you want to strive for. IKIGAI is your decision, not something imposed on you. This includes liability on your part.

WHAT IS MOAI?

In Japanese, moai alludes to a deep-rooted gathering of companions. It additionally implies a social care group that gives social, monetary, wellbeing, or otherworldly interests. The moai idea was promoted in the United States by Dan Buettner, the originator of Blue Zones. Blue Zones is an association devoted to aiding individuals to carry on with longer and better daily routines by sharing the examples of longer-experienced societies.

The term started many years prior for a town's monetary emotionally supportive network. Initially, the moai were framed to pool the assets of a whole town for undertakings or public works. If an individual required the cash flow to purchase land or manage a crisis, the main way was to raise reserves locally.

Today the thought has extended to turn out to be even more a social encouraging group of people, a social custom for the fused organization. In little Okinawa areas, companions "meet for a typical reason" (at times consistently and now and again several days every week) to blabber, experience life, and offer guidance and, surprisingly, monetary help when required. They consider these gatherings their moai.

Customarily, gatherings of around five little kids were mated and that is the point at which they focused on one another forever. As a subsequent family, they routinely met with their moai for both works and play and to pool assets.

Some moais have endured over 90 years! Regardless of whether you won't ever have a moai in the most thorough interpretation, you should in any case endeavor to have an affectionate gathering of companions and meet routinely.

WHAT IS HARAHACHIBU?

Contrasted with IKIGAI and moai, harahachi bu is really straightforward and moderately simple to apply to your life. Harahachibu is an eating routine decide that says you ought to eat until you are 80% full. Restricting your admission to near, but not exactly, immersion consumes less calories, but something like you need them. It's obvious, your cerebrum is around 10-20 minutes behind your stomach. So when you quit eating when you feel 80% full, you are full. Rehearsing harahachibu, the normal Okinawan man consumes just 1,800 calories each day, contrasted with the normal American who eats more like 2,500 calories.

Other long-life illustrations from Okinawans Researchers trust IKIGAI, moai, and harahachibu are three main reasons Okinawans live lengthy, solid lives.

Different supporters include Plant-based and exceptionally shifted diets: Okinawans eat a greater number of vegetables than the vast majority (particularly green and yellow ones), as well as entire grains, tofu, fish, and different vegetables.

They eat almost no sugar and very little meat, dairy, or eggs. In a CNN interview with Sanjay Gupta, Craig Willcox, the author of the book "Okinawa Program", clarified that Okinawans "normally eat seven distinct soil products and 18 unique food varieties per day and more than 200 consistently distinct food sources and flavors". in their general food routine.

In the United States, we are lucky to eat twelve distinct food sources in our typical everyday eating regimen, altogether ". The veggie lover diet is intrinsically wealthy in cell reinforcements, flavonoids, fiber, supplements and is normally low-calorie and calming.

Action: Staying dynamic doesn't mean running 10 miles per day or perspiring in the exercise center. The Okinawan thought of activity is to make actual work a piece of regular daily existence. Practically all Okinawans are dynamic walkers and landscapers. Cultivating is an everyday actual work that energizes a wide scope of versatility. Okinawans are likewise more inclined to strolling, cycling, and, surprisingly, taking part in combative techniques. Likewise, their homes have exceptionally restricted furnishings and they eat sitting on tatamis on the ground. Getting ready builds adaptability and strength.

Daylight: Due to their tropical climate and dynamic open-air way of life, Okinawans benefit from all-year openness to vitamin D.

22
EXERCISES TO IMPROVE YOUR IMMUNE SYSTEM

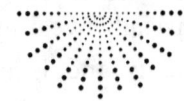

1. **Situated half spinal contort**

*I*t is the yoga that represents tenderly (delicately, it is the watchword here!) compressing, bending the spine, and in addition, invigorating the stomach. This fortifies our resistance and separates poisons that may eventually cause illness or irritation due to unfortunate assimilation.

What to do

- Sitting with your legs straight out in front of you, plant your right foot to the outside of your left leg, near the knee area so that the bottom of your right foot is on the floor.
- Keep your left foot broadened flexed.
- Plant your right palm directly behind your lower back and bring your elbow past your right knee.
- Breathe in to lift and stretch the spine, breathe out to wind, and loosen up the body.

1. **Pay attention to the sounds**

Sound and music can without much of a stretch modify your mindset and influence your psyche. All that you pay attention to turn out to be essential for yourself. Thusly it is vital to encircle yourself with sounds that satisfy you.

What to do

- Supplant the brutal hints of your morning caution with something more delicate and melodic.
- Stand by listening to playlists that incorporate hints of nature: birds, water, waves, and so on.

At the point when you are in a circumstance where there are sounds, for example, vehicle blaring, development work, gab during a busy time, and so on Rather than getting disappointed by these sounds, stop briefly and center around standing by listening to the examples the sounds produce very much like you would assume you were paying attention to music.

1. **Breathing activities**

As of late, breathing has turned into a focal point of logical exploration and studies. Legitimate breathing goes about as a method for people to assume responsibility for their wellbeing. It works on actual wellbeing and wellness execution, oversees torment, eases and forestalls illness, and influences resistance.

What to do

- Nasal Breathing: The air we take in through the nose goes through the nasal mucosa, which animates the reflex nerves that control relaxing.

- Breathe in with the stomach: this is finished by getting the stomach, a muscle found evenly between the chest cavity and the stomach depression. Air enters the lungs, the chest doesn't rise and the gut grows.

1. **Focus as an entryway to contemplation**

An uncollected and dispersed mind is something contrary to a thoughtful brain.

What to do

Concentrate on your breath. Try not to transform it or power it to be a sure way. Allow him to inhale appropriately during the second you are. Continue to observe it. On the off chance that your psyche gets occupied and begins pondering different things, let it occur, yet keep your self-control zeroed in on noticing your breath all things considered.

Keep your look consistent. Attempt to hold your eyes back from flashing or meandering in various headings. Track down a point of convergence with your look and remain there. Inhale normally as you get it done.

Carry your attention to the various region of your body parts and loosen up them utilizing your psyche. It begins at the bottoms of the feet and closures at the highest point of the head.

JAPANESE IKIGAI WORKS OUT

IKIGAI is a Japanese word that fundamentally signifies "motivation to be" in the feeling of replying "how would it be a good idea for me to manage my life?". One of the approaches to "open" your IKIGAI is with the Japanese IKIGAI works out.

It has been proposed that since the idea has its starting points in the Japanese island of Okinawa that IKIGAI might hold the way to both bliss and life span. There are numerous sites discussing this at present and the things you ought to do to "open" your "IKIGAI". Of these things, however, I just need to focus on one couple, the couple that I might have the opportunity to help you with:

- Abandon the desperation and embrace a more slow speed of life.
- Get fit with delicate, everyday work-out.

ACTIVITIES OF RADIO TAISO

Radio Taiso is a progression of standing, bodyweight just activities intended to place your joints in their full scope of movement. Joint developments are normally well beneath their full scope of movement, so the muscles can progressively ease off. You put your body through a full scope of movement every day and you can perceive how clear it is that you will keep on working better and feel better for longer.

Activities can likewise further develop readiness and stance which thus can assist with straightforward things like getting up from a seat or making headway. Also, delicate activities like these toward the beginning of the day get blood streaming around your body, which thusly will empower you, release your joints, and take out developed solidness.

I can unquestionably perceive how this could assist with IKIGAI! There are three projects in the Radio Taiso set: the first is the fundamental daily schedule, the second is for growing more strength, and the third you could do it plunking down if you need!

RADIO TAISO

Radio Taiso is a real sense signifies "radio activities" and they are a progression of basic activities from Japan. The "radio" part comes from the way that an opportunity to play out these activities is communicated on the radio. We have the 3 fundamental schedules, however, here is the principal exercise of the main daily practice:

STRETCH AND DEVELOP

By beginning with an activity to promptly work on your stance, you will adjust your body to help MORE from any remaining activities and to assist with forestalling wounds.

Center: The focus during this exercise should be on the back muscles. Think carefully if you feel your arms "straight" everywhere the same on both sides. Just do what you can every day, but think carefully about trying to work the next day. NEVER power or attempt to train a specific muscle further than necessary.

STRETCH 'N' GROW RADIO TAISO

Position 1: Stand with your impact points together and your feet about 45 degrees apart. The arms are along the edges, and the hands are grasped in lightly clasped hands. (A lightly clenched hand is a place where the fingers of the hand are curled and the fingertips simply come into contact with the palm) The sides of the clasped hands should touch the highest point of the thighs, the knuckles facing forward before. Stand as straight as possible pushing your shoulders back, pushing your neck against an imperceptible collar, and FEEL your chest rise and flow out normally and your stomach in.

Position 2: Keeping your arms straight, raise both arms in front of you until they are straight above your head. Try brushing your ears with your upper arms while you do this. Focus on the knuckles of each hand. You want to keep your knuckles as far away from you as possible throughout development. Each hand is a circle of radioactive energy that EXPLODES assuming it gets too close. At the most noticeable mark of this development, make sure your body is tense and your lungs are fairly full.

*Relaxing: breathe in as you raise your arms, breathe out as you lower them.

Position 3: With your arms still above your head, open your hands while holding your fingers together (so that the hand is fairly horizontal, similar to an oar, with the palms facing you). Without stopping, gradually lower your arms to the side until they return to the sides. Here, the emphasis is on the energy emanating from the fingertips. You have beams of energy emerging from every fingertip, except as long as your arms remain fairly straight overall.

Position 4: Same as the first position. The Radio Taiso routine just requires that this development be rehashed twice. For a normal count of four, you simply need to repeat each progression twice. I'm inclined to do this development three or more times with a slower account:

- Arms outstretched before the body (stop for the count of 4)
- Arms straight upward (stop for 4 counts)
- Arms aside (stop for the count of 4)
- Arms down aside (stop for the count of 4)

Survey: This exercise has been a startup "planning" practice for over 75 years! It fulfills an activity of direction, because it advances the position, pushes the lungs to charge with natural air. You will regularly see the consolation of playing this activity from an open window.

Variety: It's quite satisfying to start with hands at thigh level and keep hands in a "paddle" position throughout development. The palms will face each other until they come to the head, then, at that point, will turn and face down on the lead (as in the past).

23

PRACTICE TAI CHI QUAN TO INCREASE LONGEVITY

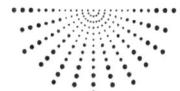

People who practice Tai Chi Quan may have various explanations behind this fact. Some may just do it as a game, others may do it for exercise, despite everything others might need to dominate a military skill. Anyway, there is another advantage of Tai Chi Quan: against maturation. When done with precision, Tai Chi Quan can extend life expectancy.

By rehearsing Tai Chi Quan, individuals can improve their unique Chi which has the impacts of fortifying the body, eliminating infections, and advancing life span because by rehearsing Tai Chi Quan they can knead all organs, broaden and stretch the spine. Furthermore, joints.

Nevertheless, assuming you take a look at people who practice Tai Chi Quan impartially and cautiously, it is clear that many people feel the adverse effects of chronic weakness and shortness of life. The current situation will not change by paying little attention to Kung Fu dominance.

In current history, there have been 36 well-known Tai Chi Quan aces in China, and their normal life expectancy was 60 years. Of the 36, there were 9 who lived under 60, showing that the leading aces who focused on their well-being while doing Tai Chi Quan saw the true impacts of lifespan.

Many individuals have had medical issues and, surprisingly, significant diseases since forever ago, yet doing Tai Chi Quan has assisted them with recuperating their wellbeing and carrying on with a more drawn-out life. Thus, we can have a total and objective comprehension of Tai Chi Quan simply by logically breaking down these cases.

Besides, we can help the developing number of Tai Chi Quan fans to find out about the various capacities and advantages of Tai Chi Quan and the various approaches to doing Tai Chi Quan to live longer.

Kendo Quan and Daoism have a similar source, which depends on the rule of vacancy. The void of Tai Chi Quan infers tranquility alongside non-activity. Through quiet and unwinding, they can get the profundity of Tai Chi Quan. By rehearsing quietness and unwinding, they are more open to tuning in and noticing. They will step by step figure out how to see that the elements of Tai Chi Quan include numerous polarities. For instance, through the apparent structures [Tai Chi Quan, action], they can appreciate the undetectable [The Dao and Wuji, non-action].

At the point when individuals practice Tai Chi Quan under the direction of Daoism speculations and methods of reasoning, they can likewise slowly comprehend that everything in the universe has circumstances and logical results and is adaptable; that is, the universe guarantees consistent change. After the peak comes the dusk, and after the nightfall comes the apex. After an activity, there is a response. After development, there is a withdrawal. After moving, there is the sinking. These dualisms are widespread realities, for which there are laws of equilibrium. At the point when individuals come to comply with these work regulations, they can follow their destiny and not feel very cheerful or incredibly miserable when conditions change. Rather than being pulled in inverse headings, individuals can figure out how to find an equilibrium [follow "the center ground"]. Living a quiet, tranquil life will build the surge of Chi inside individuals' bodies, feed their unique Chi, work on their safe framework's capacity to battle sickness, and advance life span.

You need to perceive the certainty of changes to, unwind and trust, and at last foster positive reasoning and tackle issues. The types of Tai Chi Quan guide individuals to this acknowledgment. While rehearsing Tai Chi Quan, individuals can do a profound investigation of the structures by liking these normal standards of progress and adjust as should be visible in the cooperation of Yin and Yang through the structures: slow or quick; vacant or strong, detached or forceful, etc. These associations between the Dao and nature show that the all-inclusive laws of progress are continually working. When individuals who practice Tai Chi Quan acknowledge how to continually observe the new harmony between these dualities, they can unwind, neglect, and join nature itself while decreasing pressure and overseeing life better.

Whether individuals utilize Tai Chi Quan to battle, perform or contend, they should all follow the standards of Daoism and nature, and they should neither power themselves nor show hesitance. If individuals strain exorbitantly while playing out the structures or performing them without interior strength, it will conflict with the idea of Tai Chi Quan, making the deficiency of unique Chi and harm the body. This peculiarity is found in many games contests.

To live long, one must live by the principles of physical and psychological well-being while dominating the routine [mindful, trained, and collected practice] expected in Tai Chi Quan. Whenever people who practice Tai Chi Quan only focus on building or fighting but do not stick to the inner system, they will not have the benefit of the Tai Chi Quan system. To develop inner strength, one must begin the training with vacancy and non-existence and end the training with emptiness and non-existence.

Moreover, when individuals experience vacancy and nonexistence in Tai Chi Quan, they can develop inward fortitude, yet additionally, see that they are in solidarity with the world. Consequently, they can confront the world deceitfully, experience and notice life, control the future, have a perfect existence, and not feel contacted by the addiction and misfortune, which is the vacant mentality of Tai Chi Quan. This authority, which comes from further developing the understudy's level, requires separation from life. That is, through Tai Chi Quan, individuals can figure out how to notice life's difficulties instead of responding to them. They figure out how to manage numerous unpleasant circumstances with quiet objectivity rather than being pulled in a wide range of headings. This idea is the Tai Chi Dao of life.

Jujitsu Quan is not just Chinese boxing. Since the repetition approach depends on calm and relaxation, it has a few attributes that different games do not have, which seek stability in development, seeks development in tranquility, and consider calm as the premise which gives Chi to all individuals. . With successful practice, Tai Chi Quan could have a significant impact on the mindsets of individuals by working on their personal satisfaction and duration.

Be that as it may, following the routine expected by Tai Chi Quan is a long-term challenge: the impact of society, the control of the rhythms of life of individuals, the quest for need, and the quest for combat, performance, and fighting Tai Chi Quan. These blockages inevitably mislead individuals, causing them to truly put into words the developmental standard of tranquility.

It should be remembered that the highest level of Tai Chi Quan is to achieve joy, well-being, and lifespan, to embrace the standards of stillness and emptiness, which promote the separation of wounds from life and relieve long longings. The exchange of tranquility and development in structures also advances mindfulness and soul improvement, which must be accomplished through the demonstration of self-neglect [a type of separation that advances compassion].

Having a sort and open heart is a definitive objective in Tai Chi Quan practice because an open heart is an immense ocean, where issues are nevertheless little waves. Having less pressure in life leaves more space for bliss and thusly the generosity to bloom. Consequently, moral development is likewise essential for this interaction on the grounds that exclusively supporting a sort and open heart can individuals advance great wellbeing and a long life expectancy.

CONCLUSIONS

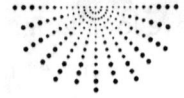

*I*KIGAI is much more than energy or a vocation. Supposing one has a reason throughout everyday life, the idea of energy makes no difference. Viewpoints can be restored by looking at the present from a future state and contrasting the current setting and the most pessimistic scenario situations. It is essential to recognize feelings of nervousness, dread, or stress; in any case, we must not capitulate to them or even try to kill them.

Attitude

People who live longer have an uplifting outlook and a serious level of enthusiastic mindfulness. They can deal with their feelings during times of mishap. Reflection "recalls the turning point" of the psyche. The treatments reinforce serenity and help to love the most important and best parts of life.

While low circulatory strain and infrequent pressure can be helpful, progressive pressure is truly destructive and can cause exhaustion, misery, sensitivity, trouble sleeping, and nervousness.

A strong funny bone and a smile at people (even strangers) also help.

Emotionlessness helps control interruptions of pleasure and desire, through balancing rather than elimination. A strong sense of strength beats obstacles and is additionally adaptable to adjust and change strategies.

"Hostile to delicacy" can be worked by making redundancies (eg numerous income streams; kinships outside of connections), spreading wagers, and diminishing slightness (eg staying away from harmful individuals, lessening computerized interruption).

Stream

Clinician Mihaly Csikszentmihalyi characterizes the idea of the stream as "the state wherein individuals are so engaged with an action that basically nothing else appears to have any significance; the actual experience is pleasant to the point that individuals will do it at an excessive cost, only for entertainment purposes."

An adequate degree of challenge upholds the vivid force of stream; a lot of prompts uneasiness, too little prompts fatigue. Making little strides all at once and developing the propensity for discipline assists with beating the squares of inactivity in the stream zone.

A solid capacity to endlessly think is expected to support the stream; separation from computerized media ("tech quick") helps here. A lot of performing various tasks and interferences can prompt mistakes, sat around idly, decreased usefulness, fatigue, a sensation of loss of control, less innovativeness, and memorable powerlessness what was finished.

Japanese experts are eminent for their steadiness (even fixation) and ingestion in their assignments, with an intense scrupulousness. "The Japanese public has a novel ability for making new advancements while safeguarding create customs and procedures," they clarify.

Steve Jobs himself loved Japanese plans in porcelain and hardware, eg. the specialist Yukio Shakunaga. The soul of "complex effortlessness" (instead of "lethargic straightforwardness") is noticeable in Japanese workmanship, design, and food. The Japanese are skilled at joining nature and innovation; not man against nature, but instead an association of the two.

It is likewise vital to safeguard one's reality to exploit IKIGAI; a specific degree of security and even forlornness is clear among numerous fruitful individuals. Routine exercises and commonplace assignments have a related "microflow": for instance, Bill Gates says he gets a kick out of the chance to wash the dishes around evening time as it unwinds and clears the psyche.

Customs likewise have their parts of the stream and help separate the major objectives into auxiliary parts. The most joyful individuals on the planet aren't the ones who get the most. They are the ones who invest more energy than others in a condition of transition.

THE LONGEST-LIVED INDIVIDUALS

Individuals of Okinawa have a solid feeling of the local area and praise the customs of life. The creators likewise suggest playing with pets or kids, as well as an adequate brandishing act. The key to a long and blissful daily routine isn't to experience the desire for an incredible life tomorrow. Today is to live with expectation. What I love is that this isn't just imaginable on a singular level, however, whole networks can gain from it also.

DID YOU TRACK DOWN YOUR IKIGAI?

www.ingramcontent.com/pod-product-compliance
Lightning Source LLC
Chambersburg PA
CBHW072056110526
44590CB00018B/3199